1001
IDEAS FOR LIVING

1001
IDEAS FOR LIVING

Bath · New York · Singapore · Hong Kong · Cologne · Delhi · Melbourne

This is a Parragon Publishing book
Copyright © 2007 Parragon Books Ltd

Parragon Books Ltd
Queen Street House
4 Queen Street
Bath BA1 1HE

Editorial coordination: Catherine Collin
Text: Cristian Campos
Photographic documentation: Cinta Martí, Julio Fajardo
Art Direction: Mireia Casanovas Soley
Layout: Ignasi Gracia Blanco

US edition produced by Cambridge Publishing Management Ltd
Translation: Leslie Kay
Editor: Catherine Senker
Proofreader: Juliet Mozley

ISBN: 978-1-4054-9534-9

Printed in China

Contents

INTRODUCTION

THE BEST TIME TO DECORATE

One of the key factors in decorating well is timing when you do it. It is best to decorate when you feel good in yourself but would like to change some aspects of your surroundings to help you improve your quality of life. The main aim of decorating is to create a pleasant and harmonious environment, and you will only be able to achieve this if you are happy at the time. If you decide to decorate a room in a period when you feel sad, this sadness will undoubtedly be reflected in the decoration itself and may influence the future in a negative way.

When decorators prepare a project, they hold long discussions with their clients, since the better the decorators understand their needs, the better the results will be. When you are the decorator, you must carry out this dialog with yourself. It is a mistake to think that you can avoid this. You must analyze objectively what your needs and preferences are and discover the possibilities offered by the space you have available. The more in-depth and detailed this analysis is, the more satisfactory the final result will be.

Another key factor is to allow sufficient time for decorating. You should conceive the process as a long and evolving phase, and be open to changes. Although at the beginning you may choose one color, for example, you may later realize it is not the most appropriate one. This is a perfectly normal part of the design process, and you should revise your choice of color. Large surfaces may change the tone of a color that you thought suitable when you first tried it out, so it may be necessary to think again. It is also worth taking your time when you are buying items to add the finishing touches to the area you are decorating.

It is a good idea to leave the decorating unfinished so you can make new additions and changes in the future. Then you will feel that your home is like a living being that evolves with you and is nurtured by your own personal experiences, while at the same time reflecting many aspects of your personality. You should have it very clear in your mind that the objective of decorating is the creation of a pleasant and satisfactory living environment, to meet your needs. Do not allow yourself to be too influenced by fashion. The best decoration is not what has cost the most money or where there are the most fashionable objects, but what makes you feel comfortable in your own home and suits your own style and tastes.

CHOOSING A STYLE

Choosing a style for your home is something very personal. Although it may seem that the easiest thing is to let yourself be guided by the images on TV or photos in magazines or books, it is important to realize that such photos reflect the styles and personalities of the people who created them. If you copy them faithfully, they will not be an expression of you yourself, but of them. This does not mean that you have to do without these sources of information, but simply consider them as an inspiration. When choosing a style, you should be aware first of the space you have available and second of the possibilities it offers you.

The architectural quality of the building is an important factor; you may choose to highlight it if it interests you or to conceal it if you prefer. At this stage in the analysis, try to look objectively at the potential of the space and the items you have available. Then you can decide what you want to retain, what to restore with a few changes, and what to eliminate completely. You might begin the process by considering a significant element, such as an antique furniture item inherited from a family member or some stained-glass windows in an old building. In cases like these, it is generally best to decorate the space to revolve around these elements. They will become the center of attention, and all the other objects you will add to complete the room will be organized around them. Once you have made this decision—which should be as objective as possible—you can then go on to choose a style.

As already indicated, TV programs, books, and magazines are an important source of inspiration. Another may be the knowledge of another culture. You could create a space inspired by Oriental, Indian, or African designs, but always bear in mind that your space should also reflect personal aspects. If you neglect to do this, you could find yourself with rooms that appear more like a museum than your own home.

The next step involves collecting samples of any type of item or material that could help you to create the style you like. Try to bring together the largest possible number of elements, including photographs, materials, plants, fabrics, and colors—anything you like. When you have a large collection, you can begin to discard the ones that do not fit your chosen style or that do not suit your possibilities. The result of this process will be a set of objects and materials that illustrate the different treatments you could choose to decorate the various spaces. With all this information gathered together, you can get started on your decorating project.

Remember that you have a very powerful resource at your disposal that will help you give more character to the environment you are creating: lighting. The lighting you choose will depend on the style you have chosen. If you want to create an 18th- or 19th-century atmosphere, it is best to opt for rather low lighting levels. In period interiors, the choice of sockets and switches is important. You may want to select ones that can be concealed easily, or install reproductions or modified original items bought from antique shops or flea markets. Some lamps have a strong character and can become an outstanding element of the decoration, evoking an atmosphere in their own right. A Tiffany Art Nouveau lamp will take you swiftly to the turn of the 20th century, while a conical green glass lampshade will create an atmosphere reminiscent of a smoke-filled Edwardian billiard room.

REDECORATING

If you want to redecorate a room, the process will be somewhat different. Redecorating is based on conserving the vast majority of the elements you already have. You will need to rearrange the elements that are already in the space and work out which decorative techniques you can use.

Although it seems difficult to change a space without introducing new elements, you will certainly be surprised at the possibilities. Keep in mind all the available decorating techniques, such as stripping or reupholstering, that allow you to completely change the appearance of a piece of furniture. During the redecorating process, you should always maintain a clear idea of the style you are seeking, since it is very easy to lose the cohesiveness between the various elements.

On the other hand, you need to consider the possibilities of transforming the space. You could alter the color of the walls by papering them or modify the appearance of the ceiling by lining it with wood. Other options include renovating the floor or covering it with carpet, or even improving the appearance of the windows with new curtains. Redecorating is more affordable than decorating, but be careful about the changes you make, especially if you are painting. You should always ensure that the changes you make are reversible; at some point in the future, you may want to restore the original appearance of a piece of furniture or a wall. If you are making improvements to an old or unusual building, try to make sure that your modifications do not impair the original style of the property.

CREATING NEW SPACES

Before setting about decorating a space, you need to take certain external aspects into consideration: the orientation and the views from it.

The windows provide the most important focus and point of interest in a room with good views. The orientation gives you an idea of how the space is lit in natural light, so you will be able to analyze the artificial lighting, materials, and colors that are best suited to the light conditions of the space. Whether you are redecorating an old room or creating the decor for a new house, you are configuring a new space, and you need to keep certain aspects in mind. Creating new spaces should always be done with the support of a plan drawn to scale. You can draw the new elements that are going to be introduced and see how they relate to each other, to find out if they meet your needs. It is important to obtain large-dimension samples of the materials or colors you plan to use, so you can consider them in the space they will occupy and check how they look in both natural and artificial light.

It is a good idea to think about where you will position the floor coverings (if there are any) and the wall coverings, and to observe how they are affected by the light when you place them in these positions. Although you are working in two dimensions on the plan, never forget that the space you are creating is three-dimensional. It is therefore advisable to prepare a drawing in perspective, applying the materials and colors you plan to use. This will give you an idea of the result you will achieve.

When you create and organize new spaces, you may need the help of an expert to advise you on the possibilities that the architecture of the building offers you, since you must always keep in mind the viability of expanding a space or reducing it according to your needs. In such cases, a professional will help you decide which walls or partitions you can modify and how much the work will cost.

If you plan to fully decorate a new house, you should proceed room by room.

Some rooms are difficult to deal with, either because they are very small or excessively large, or because they have an irregular shape. It may help you to make a list of the advantages and disadvantages of the room and consider these so you can make the most appropriate decisions.

In the case of small rooms, the best solution is usually to reduce the elements decorating it to the minimum and only install those that are indispensable; you must therefore make a detailed analysis of the needs of that space and the people who will occupy it. The homogeneity of the elements will also help you make a small room seem bigger.

A room of large dimensions can also be a problem. In this case, color or wallpaper can help you to create the sensation that the space is fuller. Try to avoid the tendency to accumulate superfluous objects. A good solution is to create more than one space in the same room. If, for example, it is a living/dining room, you can introduce a small space for reading or study, or even a second sitting area of reduced dimensions with a completely different style from the main one, with a more intimate atmosphere.

When dealing with rooms with irregular shapes, your first aim should be to unify the space. A good way to do this is to use made-to-measure furniture, which enables you to deceive the eye by making an oblique wall appear to form a right angle. Curtains located strategically can help you conceal a window that is off-center with respect to a wall.

If you find yourself having to cope with elements that you cannot do without, such as a poorly positioned pillar, you must analyze the situation and see if it is best to make it go unnoticed, by painting it the same color as the walls, or to highlight it so that it gains importance and becomes a focus of attention.

To have a clearer idea of a new space, you can separate out the elements that make it up: the content and the container. The container comprises the walls, the floor, and the ceiling, while the content is the furniture and other objects that will be part of the room. The cohesiveness and balance of the space you create are based on achieving the connection between content and container, as well as between the elements that make up each of these.

Despite having the same dimensions as the ceiling, the floor usually has a greater impact, and for this reason you should take special care when choosing the treatment you give it. If the room has a high ceiling, you can neutralize the effect by selecting a finish similar to that of the floor and the walls. A dark color can help to achieve this. On the other hand, a pale color that is different from the walls will make a low ceiling seem higher. The walls are an important part of the surface of the room. You can treat them as a decorative element in their own right with the help of wall-paper, paintings, stucco, and even wood coverings. Otherwise, you could treat them as a backdrop and decorate them in a neutral way. In this case, the furniture acquires more importance, so the procedure is appropriate in a room containing furniture of special interest, such as antiques.

In conceiving the new space, take into account the areas of circulation. These will determine the spaces where the furniture should be positioned and those that are to remain empty.

Spaces

Organizing the distribution of the space means physically arranging your rooms, furniture, and accessories in a way that is harmonious and suits your needs. Planning a rational, useful, and comfortable distribution of the space is the first step when developing an integrated interior design project for your home. Studying the horizontal and vertical planes, the dividing elements, the doors, windows, stairways, and partitions in advance will be of great help to you when optimizing the space available. Contrary to what you might think, organizing the space distribution in a home of large dimensions is no easier than in one of medium or small size. If anything, it poses different problems.

In interior design there are dozens of tricks that permit you to: enlarge the size of a room visually; unify spaces; take maximum advantage of the existing light; suggest different moods; conceal weak points in your home or enhance its attractive details, converting them into a visual focus of attention. In general, in a small house it makes sense to eliminate unnecessary partitions, uniting the different spaces and allowing the light to reach all the corners, while in medium or large houses the priorities involve integrating the various elements to ensure that the space flows in a cohesive way without sudden transitions. You should bear in mind that not all the tricks, advice, and suggestions included in this chapter are applicable to all types of homes. Each house or apartment has its own peculiarities, and what may seem like a good idea for one may not be helpful for another. Analyzing the characteristics of your home—its strong and weak points, and your needs and priorities—will help you find the most appropriate solution without having to go through the laborious process of trial and error. This chapter offers many practical examples, each accompanied by a concise explanation, for all those seeking to optimize the distribution of the spaces and structural elements of their home.

Stone is one of the most suitable materials for the floors of homes with a rustic or ethnic inspiration. The color of the walls should therefore bring to mind the colors of nature, such as ochers, chocolates, and coppers.

Combining apparently incompatible materials, such as concrete, brick, and wood, may appear to those who want to give their home a touch of the unorthodox.

Wooden baseboards make it possible to conceal and give an elegant finish to the join between a wall (or column) and the floor.

1 Restoring or redecorating does not always have to mean completely rejecting the elements of the original home. A spectacular exposed brick wall like the one in this apartment should be retained and consolidated as a key decorative element.

2 Barrel vaults (with a circular cross-section) are usually made of brick, reinforced concrete, or stone. Brick is a material with a strong personality that seeks the aesthetic spotlight.

3 Moldings cause interesting modulations of light and shade that are projected onto the furniture and surfaces of the area where they are fitted.

4 No written rule states that walls should have a uniform surface: combining a covering of plaster or any other material with areas where the stone is exposed will give dynamism to your home.

5 Furniture in a classic style, frequently over-elaborate, should be combined with elements that lighten its visual weight. In this case, the wall coverings around the windows give warmth and a natural feel.

6 If steel elements appear visually cold and reminiscent of an industrial aesthetic, they can be counterbalanced by means of white painted stone or brick walls, which will provide a more relaxed and harmonious atmosphere.

7 Irregular and imperfect finishes, like the finish on this wall, are natural, warm, and dynamic, in contrast with the cold, perfectionist finishes of high-tech interiors.

8 The ceiling of this space has been lined with boards of an artificial material that imitates the texture of cork; it contrasts powerfully with the industrial aesthetic of the floor.

9 Partitions lined with materials in attractive colors are normally used as strong decorative elements or as visual separators of the space.

10 The interior wall of unpolished stone blocks in this home contrasts strongly with the furniture and the rest of the wall coverings, giving the space a strong personality.

In this a home with an extremely modern design, the concrete finish lining the wall and breakfast bar of this kitchen serves to delimit the space and contrasts with the predominant white.

Because the stones that make up a wall are all of different shades within the same chromatic range, the light takes on spectacular and unusual reflections when projected onto them.

Functionality is not always separate from design: a stone wall insulates magnificently from both cold and heat.

A concrete wall completely streaked with horizontal fissures enables elements such as shelves or the steps of the staircase to be housed in it.

Gray is a color used to "tone down" the atmosphere of a room, so it is a good idea to compensate for it with warm materials or decoration in which some color details stand out.

7

8

9

10

1 Blue is a color particularly recommended for rural homes located by the sea or of rustic inspiration. In this example, the blue of the walls combines perfectly with the baked clay floor.

2 The open and well-lit spaces typical of urban lofts have their strongest allies in wood, iron, and other quality materials.

3 Glass block walls enable the various rooms of the home to be separated visually without hindering the passage of light.

4 Gable ceilings automatically call to mind houses in a traditional style. The color white and natural materials such as wood are therefore the most appropriate for lining the interior.

5 If structures made from sheets of the same material, positioned parallel to each other, allow the light to pass through, there will be interesting light effects in the interior of the space.

6 Printed fabric wall coverings with vertical stripes are typical of Neoclassical-inspired interiors.

7 In addition to traditional hard linings currently on the market you can find other types of materials that are little used, such as padded or spongy surfaces lined with fabric.

8 In most cases, cornices, moldings, and ceiling roses make it obligatory to opt for a Classically inspired style of decoration—hence the use of wallpapers with floral decorative motifs.

9 Dark woods tend to absorb light, so they are only suitable for large spaces with abundant natural light and without major structural obstacles that impede its passage. The combination of the ceiling covering with the matching parquet floor and vertical beams is tremendously attractive.

10 The very rough textured finish of this wall combines perfectly with the half-rustic, half-austere design of the bedroom.

If you have a well-lit home, you can choose to paint one wall or more in loud or dark colors, such as red and black, to give the space energy and reinforce the contrast between the bright finish of the floor and the industrial-style texture of the ceiling.

Besides being an excellent decorative element, an interior wall made of slate or any other similar dark stone makes a perfect surface on which you can write or draw decorative motifs, or simply make a shopping list.

The smooth textures of floors tend to visually enlarge spaces.

7

8

9

10

1 A curved interior wall can be the perfect surface for a wall covering consisting of a large-format photograph. The result is an interior of Pop Art inspiration, almost kitsch.

2 A visual contrast is achieved, among other things, by combining various materials, textures, and colors in the coverings of walls, floors, and ceilings.

3 Paneling this wall using bamboo canes gives the room a neocolonial atmosphere.

4 The walls, furniture, and decorative details of this kitchen are bathed in color, and are clearly inspired by Pop Art. To make the walls lively, strong tones have been chosen using acrylic paints.

5 The types of natural stone most used for wall coverings are slate, tumbled marble, or sandstone. In this kitchen, the oven and dishwasher have been embedded in the wall.

6 To give the walls of the various levels of this property a certain weathered and rustic air, they have been painted different colors and given a mottled finish.

7 In this space the idea has been to play with Neoclassical aesthetics by painting in strong colors and drawing an arch and a false pedestal on the walls. The pedestal houses the silhouette of a bust of Greek or Roman inspiration.

8 Brick shelves, plaster walls, and stone floors are typical of traditional Mediterranean houses. They have become popular in homes with a bohemian atmosphere.

9 The spectacular mosaics on the walls are the main attraction of this home with a clear Moorish inspiration. On the other hand, the Baroque-style lamps produce fanciful reflections of light on the walls.

10 Here a large rock has been allowed to "enter" the house and act as an extra wall in the bathroom. The slate slabs of the adjacent wall and those of the floor have been chosen so as not to distract the attention from the stone wall but rather to focus on it.

Using different materials on the floor, such as wood, ceramic tiles, or thermoplastics, can be a good solution if you need to break up large spaces visually.

Soft flooring includes materials such as rubber, cork, hide, or metal. They are normally used in modern interiors where you want to give a daring, avant-garde touch.

Floors made of artificial materials can imitate some of the characteristics of natural materials and are cheaper.

1 Floors with a granite-like appearance and neutral colors (white, black, and all the tones of gray) are easy to combine and are particularly suited to minimalist interiors.

2 Marble is one of the most elegant and resistant materials that can be used as flooring. It is a metamorphic rock, the main attraction of which lies in its fine, polished finish.

3 The marble slabs covering the wall have been arranged so that the marble forms a rhombus; this introduces a dynamic element in contrast with the uniformity of the floor covering.

4 The floor of blue mosaic pieces separates the shower area visually from the rest of the bathroom areas. The small channel that surrounds the shower allows the accumulated water to drain away easily.

5 Floors in dark colors are usually balanced with walls in pale tones.

6 Wooden parquet floors are very decorative, and their design has a significant impact on the atmosphere of the room. These floors are ideal for interiors in a classic style.

7 One variant on traditional parquet is wooden tiling made with triangular pieces, generally of different shades, which introduce a dynamic element into the floor of the room. The resulting design is more striking than that of the usual rectangular blocks, and for that reason it is suitable for contemporary interiors.

8 Stone floors are the most appropriate if you want to build some brickwork furniture.

9 The coolness of some floors can be counterbalanced using carpets with warm colors.

10 Rigid floors are more durable and resistant than flexible ones, although they are more difficult to install.

Dark floors should be reserved for large homes because they visually reduce the size of the space where they have been installed.

A dark-colored floor acts as a backdrop to make the objects and furniture placed on it stand out.

Carpeted floors are much warmer than rigid floors, but they are much more difficult to maintain and require frequent cleaning.

Floors with an iridescent surface or with pronounced veins give the space a sensation of movement and continuity. They are usually in neutral colors, such as gray or white.

Stone floors are marketed in a virtually limitless range of colors and finishes, including matt, shiny, and rough.

Reflective flooring in a bone color produces a striking effect when reflecting light, in the same way that snow does. It becomes a decorative element with a strong impact on the rest of the decoration.

Wood is a natural material that ages and alters its personality as time goes by. It requires periodic maintenance, although it is much warmer than artificial materials or cold ones such as stone.

If the floor is a color belonging to the same range as the walls and ceiling, it produces an impression of visual continuity that will make you perceive the room as a compact block. In this case, the material used for the floor imitates the effect of the fine-grained terrazzo paving.

PVC floors are the most inexpensive and usually imitate so-called "quality" materials such as stone or marble.

1 One of the less well-known qualities of wood is its effectiveness in dampening sound.

2 Silestone is a non-porous material and is very resistant to staining. However, it must be carefully maintained, avoiding the use of abrasive cleaning products.

3 Sliding panels separate the different zones of this prefabricated house. The shower area has been paved with polished pebbles that dry quickly and stimulate blood circulation in the feet.

4 Carpets are one of several types of soft floor covering. They are available in a huge range of fabrics, weaves, colors, and textures.

5 Baked clay floors are porous and for this reason it is a good idea to seal them and clean them regularly with water and detergent.

6 Exterior floors have to be particularly resistant to rain and extreme temperatures; this is why stone, whether polished or not, is one of the materials most used in this type of space.

7 A stone slab floor in various textures and colors brings out the personality of an adjacent stone wall, even more so if spotlights to project the light toward the ceiling are embedded in it.

8 The floor is one of the elements that will have the most influence on the final aesthetics of your house, so you must think very carefully about what you want from it before making a choice.

9 A floor in neutral colors is appropriate when you want to highlight another type of item—in this case, the decorative tree trunks.

10 Wood decking, consisting of boards dovetailed at the sides and ends, is normally used outdoors, although it can also be selected for interiors with a Nordic influence.

Flexible flooring is less visually plain than hard flooring, although it is usually less long-lasting because it suffers more wear and tear. It is fitted by sticking it on top of a level base layer.

PVC floors wear out very quickly, so they have to be replaced frequently. On the other hand, they offer a wide range of bright colors and finishes that can suit any decorative style.

The wide range of colors and patterns available for ceramic tiles make it possible to adopt innovative solutions, for example, the kitchen floor in this photo.

Projecting stairs, which are anchored to the wall by one of their ends without any other support, are visually lighter than a conventional staircase, although they are less safe as they don't have banisters.

1 The elliptical staircase in the photo, with its imaginative winding form, gives dynamism to the space. The projecting steps reduce its visual weight and enable the observer to appreciate the spectacular structure.

2 The visual heaviness of this metal stairway has been balanced by painting it the same color as the wall and also by using banisters made of glass panels.

3 Staircases must leave a minimum distance, as headroom, of at least 6 feet 6 inches (2 meters) between the floor and the upper level.

4 To highlight the presence of the stairway, among many other solutions, the steps can be covered with a colored carpet (purple here). The effect achieved in this case is warm and very strong.

5 The matt-finish ornamental tiles covering the risers of this staircase are a decorative element in their own right.

6 The visual impact of this stairway is minimal. The steps appear to float in the air.

7 The decision to use a half-turn staircase (consisting of two parallel straight sections, without a wellhole) or a staircase with a landing will depend on the space available, the height to be reached, and the distribution of the space that you have already worked out.

8 An original geometrical stairway with projecting steps connects the lower and upper floors of this apartment with minimalist aesthetics. The stairway also acts as a decorative element in its own right.

9 This elliptical staircase blends in with the walls around it, as it has been painted the same color. This is an appropriate solution when you want to lighten its visual weight.

10 The curved partition makes it possible to see the stairway structure, turning it into a further decorative element.

Stairways without risers allow the light to pass between the steps, so they are visually lighter than traditional staircases. In this case, the wood panel that replaces the banister reduces the luminosity gained thanks to the absence of risers.

Stairways with a pronounced slope should always have a banister or some similar element to facilitate movement up and down.

U-shaped stairways leave a wellhole of sufficient size at the base to install a few furniture items. In this case, the kitchen has been built here to exploit the space to the maximum.

Cement and metal materials tend to suggest an industrial atmosphere, as in the case of this half-turn staircase.

The visual power of the straight staircase in this photo is in contrast with the elegant minimalism of the decoration of the lounge, with its avant-garde aesthetics.

Spiral staircases are structured around a central post. In this case, the steps are attached by metal cables at the opposite end to the post.

Geometrical or spiral stairways with an open axis are less visually aggressive and more pleasing to the eye than traditional straight staircases.

1 The projecting steps of this stairway allow the light to reach the level below, which would otherwise enjoy less natural light.

2 In the area located below this staircase with projecting steps, a brickwork seat has been built that also holds the hi-fi.

3 The industrial-style metal stairway of this art gallery has a square landing, giving a powerful visual effect.

4 If the wall beside the stairway and the risers are the same color as the wall that frames them, while the treads are made from a different material (in this case wood), the visual effect will be similar to that of a stairway with projecting steps.

5 A metal bar that runs right along the banister acts as a handgrip and also as a decorative element.

6 The mottled finish of this stairway gives it an air halfway between bohemian and rustic aesthetics.

7 Spiral staircases, with steps spread around a central pole like a fan, are best for saving space. They are usually found in small houses.

8 In general, it is considered that a slope of more than 50° is inconvenient and dangerous, although stairways on ships have gradients of between 55° and 70°. The recommended slope is between 26° and 36°.

9 Visually imposing staircases must be balanced with some warm decorative detail, such as paintings or plants—unless you actually want to reinforce their impact.

10 The wall of this stairway, built in cement without supports, leaves an attractive hollow in the adjacent room that is very visually daring.

Building a platform in a space with a high ceiling enables you to gain a second level for the living space. If the floor of the platform is made of glass, it will also allow the passage of light from the upper to the lower level (and vice versa).

One way of delimiting an independent space within a larger one is to place a dais in it. In this way you avoid the need to install vertical partitions or panels for separation purposes.

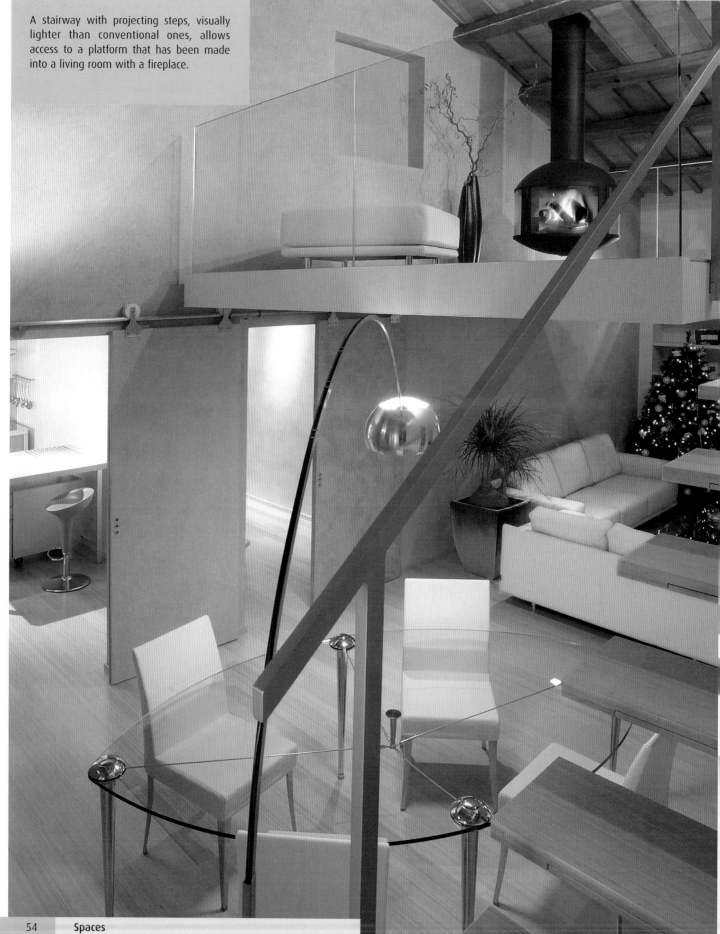

A stairway with projecting steps, visually lighter than conventional ones, allows access to a platform that has been made into a living room with a fireplace.

1 The different levels in the floor of a house can be retained using steps. Using different levels is a way of dividing the space efficiently without needing to use a dais.

2 To maintain the fluidity and cohesiveness of the lines in a room on two levels, you can opt for tables that are approximately the same height as the floor of the upper level.

3 In this case, the separation between the interior space and the external platform, located at different levels, has been underlined by means of original lighting.

4 A typical option in contemporary bedrooms is to put the double bed on a platform to make it stand out.

5 To integrate furniture located at various heights inside the same room, you can opt for a color—in this case orange—that acts as a connecting element.

6 Platforms are common in outdoor spaces, and are conceived as exterior extensions of the house. The gaps between platforms can be overcome with "bridges," and it may be a good idea to put decorative plants on them.

7 The various levels of the same room can be integrated or separated radically by the use of different coverings for the walls of the two environments.

8 The difference in levels between the floor and the platform may be a few inches; in this case, it is the same height as the dining table.

9 Cushions of different sizes have transformed this external platform into a chill-out area.

10 The wooden mezzanine in this house is supported by two iron girders and enables kitchen appliances and a lamp lighting the lower level to be hung from its crossbeams.

Many modern houses have eliminated the traditional division between the first and second level using daises and platforms, which therefore become intermediary levels and divide the space without the need for partitions.

To take advantage of the natural light entering through the high glass wall of this house, a platform has been built that houses the work zone. Without it, it would have been necessary to install this space in a less well-lit part of the house.

Beams are not solely structural elements of the home, but can also function as decorative elements. For example, they can be painted the same color as the ceiling or a different color to highlight their presence.

In houses with a Dutch roof (a form of pitched roof) the framework is usually left exposed. In this case, the crosspieces have been used to install adjustable spotlights.

The successful combination of modern and traditional elements (the naturally aged wood frame of the ceiling and pillars, of the same material) gives this large living/dining room a unique personality.

1 The beams and pillars of this house with an avant-garde design have been left exposed, together with the cramps that reinforce their union, as a further decorative element.

2 In this case the beam and the pillar on which it rests act decoratively as a frame for the room. The contrast between the aged wood of the beam and pillar and the rest of the materials in the room divides the space.

3 The joists of this space, which no longer bear any load, have been retained as a decorative element to balance the coldness of the materials chosen for the wall coverings.

4 The lattice of beams and pillars of this house acts as a decorative element in its own right.

5 The columns in this room help give it a certain symmetry, an effect reinforced by the positioning of the dining table in the center of the room.

6 The two metal columns that separate the kitchen area from the living room are, together with the beam they support, the only element that this apartment retains of its original configuration. They are genuine decorative master cards.

7 The mixture of elements with a raw rustic personality, such as the wooden pillars of this lounge, along with other entirely contemporary ones, is increasingly common in today's urban homes.

8 Several columns positioned in a line will help give the space visual depth.

9 The industrial aesthetics of these pillars, with the enormous rivets along their shafts left exposed, perfectly combine with the cool palette of colors in the room.

10 From the decorative perspective, pillars are usually extraneous elements, although they can also act as strong visual contrasts that give hardness and personality to an excessively soft space.

Painting the cross-shape of the pillar in the photo red makes it easy to see the spaces and levels into which the house is divided. In this way the wall acts as a visual dividing element.

The brick pillars joined as arches across the ceiling have survived the restoration of the space, this becoming the focus of visual attention.

This structure of cross timbers with a rustic appearance creates an almost sculptural piece that helps separate the bathtub from the rest of the bathroom.

The angled metal columns of this room give it dynamism and break with the traditional proliferation of vertical and horizontal lines in contemporary interiors.

A wood panel separates the dining area from the living room. As it only reaches eye level, it does not obstruct the passage of light and is less obtrusive than a conventional partition.

This attractive vermilion-colored panel acts as a dividing axis for various spaces in the house. A built-in spotlight in its lower part lights the adjacent area and highlights its presence.

Two sheets of printed translucent methacrylate that hang by clamps from the upper level act as space dividers. However, they do allow light to pass through and also act as decorative elements.

Three translucent glass panels screen the dressing area from the bedroom. Their presence goes practically unnoticed, as they merge with the neutral tones chosen to decorate the bedroom.

1

2

3

4

5

6

1 A panel on wheels enables you to divide up the space however you like, depending on your requirements.

2 Transparent dividing panels acquire an ethereal personality if they are lit from below using adjustable spotlights built into the floor.

3 Frosted glass is one of the materials most used in the manufacture of translucent dividing panels.

4 The reflective surface of this interior partition visually expands the surface area of the bedroom. Its bluish tone gives the room an attractive decorative detail.

5 This panel acts as a banister on the upper level, where the main bedroom of the house is located. The aperture allows the passage of light and the people in bed to see what is happening on the lower level.

6 A panel with an irregular outline such as the one in the photo gives dynamism and an organic touch to the room where it is located.

7 In this greenish-colored methacrylate panel, a television has been embedded on a pivoting axis, enabling it to be turned so it can be seen from either of the rooms.

8 A decorative panel may be the ideal space to hang a work of art or a large-format painting to give personality to the room.

9 Vinyl sheets are frequently chosen for decorating partition panels.

10 A small, discreet folding screen with an imaginative shape acts as a space divider and becomes a further decorative element in itself—almost a sculpture.

Red light is filtered through the sheets of the curved panel in the photo, becoming a visual focus for the house. The final effect is almost futuristic.

A simple red painted partition separates the bedroom from the kitchen. The baseboard, gray in color and with a granite texture, connects the partition visually with the floor, avoiding an abrupt break.

Movable partitions or panels enable you to modify the size and distribution of the rooms of your home at will, simply by moving them from one side to the other when necessary.

This partition is inspired by the lattice wood and rice-paper walls of traditional Japanese houses. Its curved shape generates a visual sensation of movement.

1 By leaving the space between their upper edge and the ceiling free, these partitions allow the room to "breathe" visually. Partitions separate the bedroom from the bathroom.

2 The bedroom of this apartment is separated from the rest of the room by means of movable white MDF panels on one side and polished glass panels on the other.

3 In this example, the panel acts as a headboard for the bed and as a separator; behind it is the couple's dressing area.

4 A bluish-colored folding screen, painted as though it were Venetian stucco, becomes a decorative element in the house.

5 This is an original way to integrate the garage into the house: by installing a glass partition that allows you to see the car from the dining room. This is a very visually daring solution.

6 Bright colors such as red focus the visual attention on the panel or partition instead of on the elements that surround it.

7 Two translucent glass panels installed on metal bars allow the TV to be hidden away when it is not being watched.

8 In this house with a contemporary style, distinctions between partition and window are lost in the case of this panel separating the dining room from the living room. Being fitted with glass, it almost acts as a large frame around the adjacent room.

9 Four wooden sheets hung from a guide rail by means of clamps act as space separators, but they are visually less aggressive and invasive than a conventional partition.

10 Partitions for the wet area of the bathroom must be made of a material that is resistant to humidity and high temperatures.

Standing a few inches above the floor, this translucent glass panel is less heavy visually than a conventional partition.

The glass wall that houses this door, also made from glass, allows the passage of light and visually lightens the partition into which they are fitted.

Sliding doors are an excellent space saver, especially if they have a chamber and can be concealed in a hollow in the wall. They can be curved to fit the shape of the wall or the structure that houses them.

Doors with panels made of paper, glass, or any other material are visually lighter than solid wood.

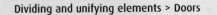

The sliding door of this room has a wooden frame, which reinforces the sensation of visual continuity with the ceiling and floor. The door slides on a glass partition that serves as an inactive pane.

This solution is midway between a sliding door and a movable partition. It allows spaces to be separated or connected at will, depending on the requirements of the moment.

In houses in a Classical style, the frames or architraves of the doors are usually decorated with moldings or engraved in relief with ornamental Greco-Roman motifs, just like pediments.

Doors with moldings require more complex cleaning care than flat doors.

A simple revolving door that swings on a central pivot will allow a more fluid circulation between the two rooms. Visually, it appears as though the two spaces have been separated by a movable partition rather than by a conventional door.

Slatted doors, made from strips of wood or any other material, allow the circulation of air but not of light, unless the slats are fitted to allow a small amount of space between them.

The combination of khaki green and a natural wood color in this room gives it a bohemian and relaxed atmosphere.

1 This is an original solution for a trapezium-shaped door: three triangular leaves, two active swinging ones, and one inactive one, which fit together. The central leaf has been fitted upside down, that is, it is shaped like an inverted triangle.

2 The glass doors inserted into partitions of the same material usually have glazing bars (wooden or metal elements that act as a frame for the glass leaves) to emphasize their presence and make sure they are noticed.

3 A paneled door allows a wardrobe to be created, taking advantage of a "dead" end of the room.

4 The paper doors and wooden latticework glazing bars typical of traditional Japanese houses have been adopted by Western designers for use in their projects.

5 The orange-tinted glass of the door of this bedroom acts as a counterpoint to the bluish tone of the window.

6 Metal carpentry is rather more economical than wood and is the most appropriate for decorating interiors in a contemporary style.

7 A striking option for a modern environment: a sliding metal door with a decorative gold band or central panel.

8 Taking advantage of all the light available may require a glass partition like this one, which houses a door, obviously also made of glass.

9 These sliding doors have practically no visual impact; because they are white, they integrate into the wall that houses them.

10 Painting doors in bright colors is a daring but valid decorative option if, for example, you want to mix materials with very different colors and aesthetics.

This sliding door is mounted on a partition. The fact that both are white allows the presence of the door to be concealed when it is open.

You can buy handles of all types, to fit with practically any decorative style. When opting for one or another, you should take into account that the handle determines to a large extent the aesthetics of the door.

Two spotlights embedded in the ceiling make it possible not only to light the door zone but also, if it is made of glass, to play with different light effects. For example, you can install colored bulbs.

Large hinges and handles reinforce the imposing presence of this wooden double door. This option is only advisable for large spaces with rough aesthetics.

Elements with a powerful personality attract the gaze, but distract attention away from everything that surrounds them.

The design of the original closing system of this sliding door and the handle, together with the industrial aesthetics of the panels lining the walls, give the overall effect of a safe.

MAN RAY

By painting the wall, door frame, and door red, the size of the whole area has been increased visually. Red is a color that gives a sensation of "advancing" when it is used on large surfaces.

The internal shutters of this house open by folding them toward the ceiling, to which they are attached using an anchoring system. Their wooden slats allow fine rays of light to pass through them, giving them an aesthetic association with Venetian blinds.

The roller blinds you can see in the photo hang in front of the handrail of the small balcony. They retain some of the heat, preventing it from entering the interior of the home, and filter the light coming in through the window.

Venetian blinds are made of strips of metal, wood, or fabric. They can generally be adjusted to control the amount of light entering the room.

Roller blinds are available in all heights and widths, so they are suitable for both windows and glass doors.

The blinds with slats in this living room make it possible to adjust the amount of light coming through the windows, but you can also see outside; they are not aesthetically intrusive and do not make the room feel claustrophobic.

o-measure blinds are generally
xpensive than ready-made ones,
h the adaptability of blinds makes
uitable for every decorative style.

Slatted or Venetian blinds can be installed both inside and outside the window. If they are installed outside they will retain some of the heat and keep the interior cooler.

1 Roller blinds can be made with all kinds of fabric, so they are appropriate for all types of interiors.

2 Curtains can make perfect dividing walls between different spaces inside the same room.

3 Blinds with wide slats are aesthetically more striking than those with thin slats, so their visual effect will be stronger.

4 Interior blinds can help to divide or connect spaces, depending on whether they are open or closed.

5 This curtain acts as a screen for the projector positioned in front of it. This is an original solution that energizes the space.

6 The darker a curtain is, the less light will enter the room through it, although the thickness of the fabric and its level of transparency also influence this.

7 Curtains that drop to the floor instead of falling a few inches above it will give the space a very bohemian and relaxed atmosphere.

8 In this case, hanging the curtain at a conventional height, despite the fact that the window is much lower than normal, helps give the sensation of spaciousness.

9 Sliding curtains enable you to regulate the passage of light as it varies throughout the day.

10 White curtains and blinds give the space purity and make any colored item stand out much more.

Curtains are an original and spectacular alternative to the traditional dividers (partitions, panels, floors, and traditional furniture). In the case of this loft, the curtains frame the dining space.

The tops, ruffles, and the drops of the various fabrics must be kept in mind when choosing curtains. Translucent fabrics allow the light to pass through and give an exotic and mysterious air to the room.

The curtains may be in the same color range as the furniture or the coverings or introduce an element of contrast. This is an example of a monochrome approach.

Curtains are not always drawn to one side. Some models are folded back onto themselves, vertically, imitating the folds formed by the petals of a flower.

Foldable roller blinds are very convenient. Also, when they are pulled up, they allow in light across the whole width of the window, an advantage over curtains that are drawn to the sides.

Some fabrics are just the right weight to allow light to pass through, while preserving the intimacy of the space.

Fabrics made of natural fibers, such as cotton, silk, or linen, are generally more expensive than synthetic ones such as acrylic or nylon. Midway between the two are fabrics made from artificial fibers, which are chemically treated natural fibers.

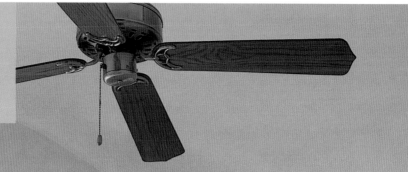

The choice of fabric for the curtains or for some cushions usually depends to a large extent on the amount of light available. In this case the curtains and the pillows are made from the same fabric, giving the room an aesthetic unity.

An alternative to the typical canopy is a translucent fabric that hangs diagonally over the bed from a bar positioned to one side of it.

The bars of the curtains can be bent around to cover "dead" corners. When the curtain is drawn back in this room, the window is completely clear, without a single inch of fabric blocking the passage of light.

A wooden piece of furniture that acts as a dining table and a worktop for the kitchen, while also housing the hob and sink, can help save precious space in small loft apartments.

In this loft, with no partitions or separating elements, the various areas have been differentiated by alternating the colors black and white: the kitchen is white, the dining table black, and the sofas in the lounge are white.

To differentiate between the various areas into which a single space is divided, you can use colors, materials, or subtle details. Here, the ceiling has been lowered by a few inches to mark the boundaries of the kitchen and also to house built-in spotlights.

The combination of built-in spotlights in both the ceiling and the floor gives the space a theatrical feel. The light beams meet in the middle to produce an attractive gleam on the surfaces of the walls or the furniture.

White surfaces give a sensation of breadth and blur edges. They also act as a canvas against which any decorative detail or furniture item will stand out, reinforcing its presence.

The bar and the two pendant lamps positioned over it separate the kitchen area and the dining room from the lounge of this apartment. However, the black color of the wall unifies them visually.

1 To light very elongated spaces or corridors, it is sensible to opt for rows of lamps positioned across the ceiling.

2 In this house, the height of the ceilings has made it possible to separate the living room area from the kitchen and dining room by raising it well over a foot above them. It appears as if the living area is on a dais or stage.

3 It is best not to position the dining room furniture too close to the working area of the kitchen in order to avoid stains and to ensure you have as much work space as possible in the kitchen.

4 A square worktop island in the kitchen, around which you can move comfortably, allows you to make the most of the space available and avoid "dead" corners. Aesthetically, this is an avant-garde solution.

5 In elongated kitchens where it is not possible to position the furniture in a U- or L-shape (the most typical), you should opt for a parallel arrangement, leaving a space or central corridor that is wide enough for you to be able to work in comfortably.

6 In open-plan spaces, the kitchen should be located as far as possible from the bedroom.

7 In the kitchen, the sockets should be located as close to the work area as possible. In this apartment, the cook can see the lounge area and the television.

8 A very well-lit room allows you to choose dark materials for your worktops. In this case, the island and the housing for the glass-ceramic hob are practically identical, giving unity to the kitchen area, which opens onto the main room of the loft beyond the marble-lined partition.

9 This red lacquered furniture item, inspired by typical Swiss army knives, houses most of the indispensable commodities in an apartment: the kitchen range, the sink, the basic appliances, and good storage space.

10 This kitchen, open to the living room, makes perfect use of the awkward space by the stairwell.

A built-in kitchen makes it possible to save precious space and frees up the central area, gaining space for the other elements in the room.

The wooden floor of this home visually unifies the kitchen space with the lounge and dining room, while the island and the various wall coverings act as separators.

In this loft with industrial aesthetics, wood has been chosen for the kitchen furniture to compensate for the visual harshness of the beams and the metal stairway that can be seen at the back of the room.

Combining two or three different types of wood is not necessarily a bad idea, provided this choice has a clear purpose. In this case, the different woods separate the kitchen visually from the dining room. The dark wooden bar, made from the same wood as the kitchen furniture, reinforces this separation.

Fanlights or lantern windows, located very close to the ceiling, allow light to fill adjacent spaces in the home that do not enjoy good natural lighting.

Islands enable you to work with great comfort and freedom of movement, and mean you do not have to cook with your face to the wall. However, they are not advisable in small or poorly-lit kitchens.

Storage items below islands are usually closed, although in some cases they are open, like this white wood island. When they are open, they usually function as decorative elements.

Islands require uniform lighting that does not leave dark areas on the surface of the worktop. This can be provided by two symmetrically positioned lights.

The extractor hood over the island should be strong, particularly if the ceiling is high, and should be located at a sufficient height above the worktop to avoid banging your head. A minimum distance of 2 feet 6 inches (75 cm) between worktop and hood is usually recommended.

This unusual island is in the form of a hemisphere, and its drawers open like the petals of a flower. A bar anchors the island to the ceiling.

The design of this original extractor hood in the shape of a tube combines perfectly with the cold, industrial, avant-garde aesthetic of the island that it accompanies.

Islands generally house the hob, the sink, and a workspace that can vary in size. In this case, the hob area has been located close to the auxiliary table that you can see in the background.

1 Placing the sink and the hob area on one side of the island leaves the rest of the space free to use as a dining table or working area.

2 Placing the island diagonally in the space means that the various areas are not as clearly separated as they would be if the island had been placed parallel or perpendicular to the units. This breaks the monotony.

3 In general, the hob should be located on the part of the island closest to the refrigerator and sink, near to the closets where the plates, pots, and pans are stored.

4 The working area of a kitchen should have powerful and uniform lighting, with no dark areas.

5 U-shaped kitchens are the most appropriate for housing an island, provided there is enough space. In this way you reduce the distance you have to move around the kitchen to a minimum.

6 In this case the sink area—where dirty plates, pots, pans, and cutlery usually accumulate—is concealed by pots for growing mint, basil, parsley, and other useful herbs for the kitchen.

7 The attractiveness of this kitchen island lies in the uniformity of the wood and an interesting and daring feature—you can insert the benches inside it.

8 A translucent glass barrier at the edge of the working area of this island protects the space around it from stains.

9 Opting for some striking wooden blocks instead of the more conventional stools has given this kitchen the impact it lacked.

10 The dark, laminated wood transforms the island into a discordant element of the kitchen design, providing a very effective color contrast.

The kitchen space, in an elegant metallic black color, is connected with the rest of the home by means of a large open window with several built-in spotlights.

The colored and indirect lighting of this space gives it warmth. The spotlights in the floor highlight the edges of the furniture items and give them a theatrical atmosphere, while those in the ceiling illuminate them.

The workspace of a kitchen is usually higher than a dining table, so stools are a good solution that allows you to integrate both in a single piece of furniture.

The sheeny finish of the metal plate that separates the dining room from the kitchen creates a sensation of movement and contrasts powerfully with the exposed brick of the wall that supports it.

An open-plan kitchen like the one in this house allows the light entering through the windows to reach the center of the dining room and the living room.

A bar with wheels can be easily moved to different areas of the kitchen or dining room, enlarging these spaces or making them smaller, depending on your needs at the time.

The materials define the various areas of this space: a dark wood for the dining room and the table, and a paler one for the worktop of the bar.

An original system of modules that fit together as though they were an architectural children's puzzle makes it possible to have a table or auxiliary bar and a bench to sit on.

Metals such as aluminum are appropriate for kitchens and bathrooms because of their toughness and resistance, but they may appear cold. You can balance them with decorative details or warm materials such as wood.

Built-in ovens save space. Positioned at eye level, they are easy to clean.

A plastic panel is appropriate for the kitchen work zone because it is tough and easy to clean. Thanks to its attractive color, it can also act as a decorative element.

1 The drawer handles on this set of kitchen units are practically imperceptible. The white surfaces extend smoothly across the kitchen and give a very stylized appearance.

2 Radical decorative options like this have to be implemented in full, otherwise they run the risk of appearing half-hearted. In this case, even the refrigerator and air-conditioning system have been painted.

3 Kitchens built into furniture have the advantage that they can be concealed simply by closing a door or a blind.

4 The worktop, wall, and shelves of this kitchen have been painted in dark gray, which reinforces the "built-in" effect.

5 Incorporating panels in totally different colors helps to radically differentiate the kitchen space when it is integrated into another room.

6 Kitchen utensils can become an additional decorative element if they are left on display. Another advantage is that you can find them easily without having to search in drawers or closets.

7 The extractor does not have to be a large structure. In this kitchen, a medium-diameter tube has been used, an aesthetically less obtrusive solution than the traditional extractor hood.

8 Scandinavian style avoids the coldness of contemporary minimalist interiors by opting for wood, generally with pale tones. Its main characteristic is its functionality.

9 Decorative details like this table leg make the space cheerful and break the barrier that separates classic styles (Provençale and rustic) from the more color-oriented ones (Pop Art and Fusion).

10 Covering the high closets in a kitchen with mirrors can be a good solution if you want to make the room seem more spacious.

Kitchen units that contain all the necessary appliances built in are convenient and very practical. It also means they do not spoil the effect of the decorative style in the rest of the home.

The combination of materials and textures in this kitchen is no more than a visual trick to give it dynamism and to avoid the tedium of monochrome or excessively sober interiors.

The open shelves for storing the crockery are very convenient, but they allow dust to settle much more easily than closets.

A discreet sliding panel on guiderails enables this kitchen to be concealed from sight when it is not being used and create a bright space.

Minimalist kitchens such as the one in the photo have minimum impact and are suitable for urban apartments with a single occupant.

An integrated unit with built-in elements can house the kitchen and the hi-fi as well as open shelves for decorative items.

1 The square holes in the wall of this kitchen are used instead of shelves for the kitchen equipment. The utensils can be beautifully displayed as decorative elements.

2 The L-shaped configuration is one of the most common in kitchens. In this case, the items of furniture have been placed symmetrically to make the room balanced.

3 Bars or peninsulas make it easy to move the crockery or food from the kitchen to the dining room.

4 Modular furniture, such as the item containing the oven and hob in this photo, can easily be moved from one corner of the kitchen to another according to your requirements.

5 Going without doors on the closets or storage drawers and leaving the dishes visible is a modern and convenient aesthetic option.

6 Lining the wall adjacent to the worktop with the same type of metal surface will offer interesting reflections if it is lit correctly.

7 Greenish colors in combination with natural materials such as stone give the room a sense of calm, as well as a clean and fresh atmosphere.

8 Choosing elements with metal finishes, like the oven and stool in the photo, is an option that combines marvelously with dark cement coverings.

9 Exposed brick walls are visually spectacular but they are dark, so it is a good idea to compensate for this disadvantage with good lighting. The glass block wall in the background enables the available natural light coming from the adjacent room to be utilized to the maximum.

10 The combination of wood and aluminum or stainless steel is a valid option for those who have opted for a traditional or rustic decorative style but do not want to do without the convenience of more modern materials.

Overcrowding the space with items can saturate it, so it is a good idea to relieve the visual weight by focusing attention on other types of detail, such as the wall coverings, the floor, or the moldings on the ceiling.

Kitchens with L-shaped modules are the best option when you want them to occupy a corner and leave space free in the rest of the room.

A crossbeam can be used to hang glass shelving for vases or other decorative objects.

Marble is a hard-wearing material that is easy to clean, so it is especially suitable for kitchens.

Abundant natural lighting enhances a space and gives it impact. Artificial lighting should serve as a complement, but never, if possible, as a basic or sole source of lighting.

8

1 In houses where priority is given to austerity and the purity of lines, it may be a good idea to build ovens and other electrical appliances into the same piece of furniture that houses the storage areas, keeping the kitchen is as clear as possible.

2 The discreet circular hood of this kitchen barely interferes with the decoration of the room.

3 Covering the doors and drawers of the kitchen with different colors and types of wood is an original and daring choice that creates a warm environment.

4 Coverings and metal appliances blend perfectly with kitchens where white is prevalent or there are translucent surfaces.

5 Lantern windows or lateral fanlights make it possible to take advantage of natural light to illuminate large spaces.

6 The gable wall, the triangular upper part of the wall at the end of a gable roof, usually becomes a wasted space. The owners of this apartment have resolved this by painting it a bright blue color and hanging a reindeer skull from it.

7 If you have a very high ceiling, it may be a good idea to install closets that use the whole vertical space. You can access them using a ladder similar to those in libraries.

8 In small kitchens with low ceilings, it is a good idea to fit one or more mirrors to give a sensation of depth.

9 The kitchen utensils are hung from a wrought-iron rack over the working area, so they are readily available for use.

10 The imaginative forms of the flecks embedded in a marble worktop can become the highlight of the kitchen if the worktops are appropriately lit.

Square shower bases usually measure around 32 inches (80 cm) per side, although larger and smaller bases exist for specific needs.

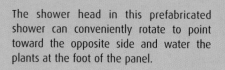

The shower head in this prefabricated shower can conveniently rotate to point toward the opposite side and water the plants at the foot of the panel.

A masonry sill built beside the shower can be used to store gels, shampoos, and other body-care products.

The main attractions of this shower are the bright colors of the walls and the stone slabs used for the floor.

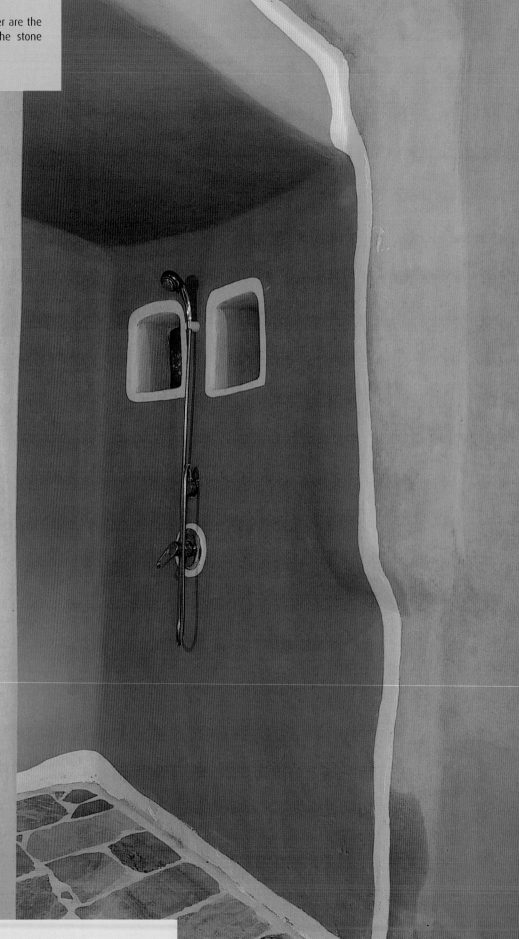

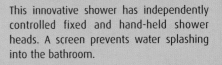
This innovative shower has independently controlled fixed and hand-held shower heads. A screen prevents water splashing into the bathroom.

Open bathrooms or those integrated into the bedroom have become popular, particularly in recent years. However, it is still sensible to enclose the shower with glass screens to avoid splashing the surrounding furniture and objects.

The shower here has a glass door to separate it from the rest of the bathroom—as if it were a separate room. This is an elegant and attractive solution if you have enough space.

1 Glass mosaics are reminiscent of those of ancient Rome, so they are suitable for bathrooms in a Classical style.

2 Modern shower columns can have a fixed shower head or a movable one, which is more convenient for the user.

3 The majority of current shower bases are manufactured with non-skid finishes to prevent slipping.

4 A completely open shower can offer an alternative to traditional closed showers in bathrooms with avant-garde aesthetics like the one in the photo.

5 The shower should be at least 28 or 32 inches (70 or 80 cm) per side—to enable you to move comfortably.

6 Screens prevent splashes, although they require careful maintenance. The most common ones consist of a fixed plate and a door or sliding panel. In this case, the fixed plate of the screen is supported by a low wall. There is a narrow space at the top to prevent the accumulation of steam.

7 The stone partition on which the shower column is fitted stretches toward the garden, perfectly connecting the internal and external spaces.

8 This original shower is part of a module with built-in closets for the storage of bathroom and body-care products. Its color aesthetics fit the space like a glove.

9 A wooden bathtub in a traditional style, but updated, can become the fun detail in a modern bathroom.

10 Stone floors are appropriate for showers because they are resistant to humidity and dry quickly.

Open bathrooms, where all the items are in view and there are no partitions or other separating elements, are a modern and suitably unconventional option for contemporary homes.

Even if you opt for an open bathroom, the toilet should be concealed from view by a partition or screen to preserve privacy.

If a room that has an open bathroom is not sufficiently well prepared to cope with water and humidity, you may have problems with damp.

1 Combining elements and furniture with differing aesthetics gives the bathroom a contemporary and eclectic atmosphere. Leaving the piping exposed can be a further decorative feature.

2 Free-standing bathtubs are an advisable option only if you have a large bathroom.

3 The design of this bathroom combines curved surfaces (the bathtub, shaped like a truncated egg, and the convex wall on the left) with straight lines and strong shapes.

4 A masonry bathtub dug into stone, reached using steps, can become one of the major attractions in the bathroom and the home.

5 To conceal this original bathtub from sight, a curtain completely surrounds it. The curtain hangs from guiderails installed in the ceiling, like a canopy.

6 So as not to break the visual continuity of the sloping walls of this attic, the closets and structures that house the bathtub have been built on an incline. The result is an avant-garde bathroom with sharp edges.

7 A radically original option: to install the bathroom in a totally independent space that is supported, like a platform, on columns. Access is gained via a stairway.

8 This wooden vat functions as a bathtub and a shower base at the same time. The design is in radical contrast with the aesthetics of the rest of the bathroom.

9 This bathtub forms a visual unity with the structure that houses it because it is built with the same material. It is a more harmonious option than traditional bathtubs built into marble or stone structures.

10 To frame this bathtub, a platform has been built that is 6 feet 6 inches x 9 feet 9 inches (2 x 3 meters) square and 28 inches (70 cm) high. Access is gained by climbing a few steps. The bathtub has been separated visually from the rest of the bathroom by means of a glass screen.

Free-standing bathtubs are visually much more spectacular than traditional ones, although they require specific installation work for the waste pipes and, in some cases, the faucets.

Oval baths are more comfortable for users than rectangular ones, as they have no right angles.

A narrow shelf around the bathtub is the ideal place to stand decorative elements or bathroom products. These have to be objects that are relatively resistant to humidity.

Contemporary design has definitively reached the bathroom. In this case, the bathtub has been built into a rectangular frame that seems to hold it in the air, although in fact it is standing on a metal base that also conceals the waste pipe.

A rectangular column houses both the mixer faucet of the bathtub and the shower hose. This is a flexible solution that keeps them away from the parts of the bathtub where users rest their head and feet.

The towel hanger should always be positioned as close as possible to the bathtub, but not so close that the towels will get wet.

1 Spectacular lighting—concealed, blurred, and colorful—gives this bathtub with futuristic features its personality.

2 Bathtubs by industrial designers are more expensive than regular ones, but they become excellent decorative elements.

3 Triangular bathtubs (with one of the tips of the triangle truncated) allow the space to be exploited better. In this case, the space has been used to install a dais that functions as a step or shelf.

4 Decorative bamboo canes endow any bathroom with freshness and vivacity. They can also be used as a separator element.

5 A circular jacuzzi has been installed on a platform with a metal structure and protected by a metal handrail, taking advantage of the spectacular height of the ceiling in this house.

6 Tiles are one of the materials most used in the bathroom. These brown ones give the bathroom an elegant, masculine atmosphere.

7 A perfect solution for a bathroom of very small dimensions: the stone surface where the washbasin has been installed reaches the wall and also functions as a shelf for bathroom and shower products.

8 A transparent glass panel offers visual continuity between the bedroom and the bathroom, so you can relax in the bathtub with the sensation that it is inside the bedroom.

9 Some bathtubs have small rubber tips to avoid slipping.

10 Surrounding the bathtub with tiling of the same color is an original way to give visual continuity to a bathroom in a classic style.

The irregular and imperfect finish of a bathtub built with ceramic or marble tiles is ideal for striking interiors with a rustic or traditional inspiration.

Positioning the bathtub under a window allows you to enjoy the views while taking a relaxing bath.

The weathered iron of this free-standing bathtub breaks the calculated aseptic coldness of this bathroom with its pure lines and Zen atmosphere.

Rustic style is characterized by its harshess and austerity, yet this does not rule out the use of color. This washbasin on legs fits in perfectly with the classic style suggested by the floor and the finish of the walls.

Rustic style frequently involves wood, particularly walnut and oak, and irregular and rather rough finishes — like that of this wall with a cavity housing the washbasin.

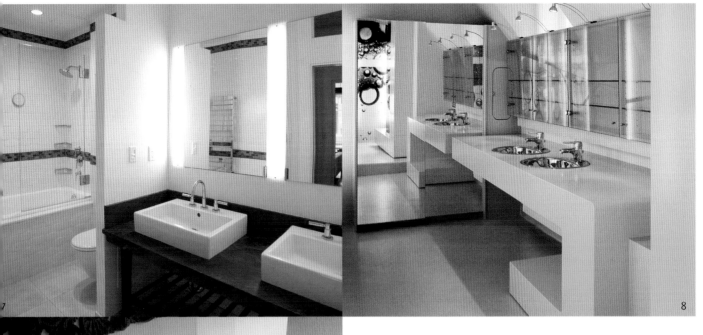

1 This piece of furniture, built with two different types of marble, has a washbasin with a tremendously original form. A dark color has been used for the work surface while the washbasin itself is pale.

2 This original washbasin decorated with black and white stripes creates a striking avant-garde contrast in a bathroom dominated visually by the harshness of the granite-like appearance of the wall.

3 Blue is associated with hygiene and cleanliness. It is therefore appropriate for bathrooms, provided it is combined with white elements or coverings, such as the elegant washbasin with legs and gold-colored faucets in this photo.

4 Wood is a warm material that immediately brings nature to mind. In this bathroom, two different types of wood have been combined, one with a rustic and another with a smooth finish. The combination goes extremely well with the rustic finish of the copper washbasin.

5 Nowadays, it is not unusual to see furniture in bathrooms manufactured using materials that were extremely rare in interior design a few years ago, such as granite, aluminum, or glass. However, they are all resistant to humidity and extreme temperatures.

6 If you opt for items with striking colors of Pop Art inspiration, such as this two-color washbasin, the bathroom should also have good lighting to prevent your skin from taking on strange tones when you look in the mirror.

7 Having two separate areas in the bathroom is much more convenient than one space with a single washbasin.

8 Bright colors cause visual fatigue, so it is advisable to balance them with items in neutral colors, such as the metal finish of these washbasins.

9 Minimalism favors order over superfluous decorative details, hence its preference for basic geometrical forms and its rejection of Baroque style and striking colors.

10 Washbasins with rustic aesthetics give a certain harshness to bathrooms decorated in neutral tones.

A washbasin made of glass or any other transparent material lightens the space visually, so it is particularly suitable for small bathrooms.

Positioning a mirror behind a washbasin is convenient and allows light to be reflected all around the bathroom.

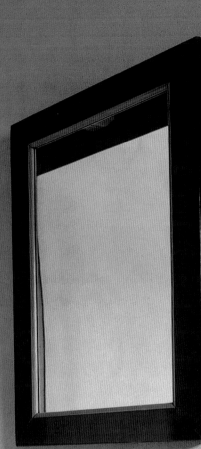

A wooden table can act as a perfect and original replacement for a traditional surface to support a washbasin in a rustic style. Its large size also makes it a convenient and functional option.

A washbasin that stands on an item of furniture conceals pipes and offers an elegant and discreet appearance to the bathroom as a whole.

1 Leaving the pipes of the washbasin exposed may be an aesthetic expedient in minimalist-inspired interiors. The built-in spotlight in the floor illuminates the washbasin area.

2 The bathroom is one of the few spaces in the home where you can freely use bold colors on the walls without the result being visually oppressive. The white of the washbasin acts as a counterbalance to the audacious brightness.

3 The glass walls of this bathroom allow you to observe the spectacular snow-covered landscape outside while using the washbasin.

4 In minimalist style, the few decorative elements acquire a fundamental importance because they are completely exposed; you can see the essential bareness of this elegant washbasin.

5 In addition to its attractive gold finish, fixing the washbasin to the wall is a successful choice in this small bathroom.

6 Ceramic mosaics consist of small tiles made of porcelain, or vitrified or unvitrified clay. These lively finishes can cheer up the environment of a simple washbasin.

7 Translucent or frosted glass doors allow you to take advantage of the light from adjacent rooms while preserving a sense of privacy at the same time. If a washbasin of the same material is fitted, the combination is very attractive.

8 A washbasin positioned lengthwise, like the one hidden behind the low wall, must have a sufficiently wide passage alongside to allow comfortable movement.

9 Placing the washbasin at the end of a long worktop leaves a large space for cosmetics and body-care products and offers a truly original configuration.

10 This original faucet and metal washbasin focus the spectator's visual attention on a single aspect of the bathroom.

In bathrooms that are to be used by two (or more) people, it is possible to opt for two separate washbasins, but also for a single large unit that houses two independent faucets, which is a useful space saver.

Materials such as slate, marble, aluminum, and stainless steel are increasingly being used in modern bathrooms. The new materials allow new shapes, designs, and colors.

At the moment it is possible to find all types of toilets on the market. Some of them go practically unnoticed, almost becoming an extra decorative element.

The rounded forms of these white bathroom fixtures make a good contrast in this bathroom, with its predominant use of right angles.

Combinations of simple and modern forms for bathroom fixtures with some classic elements, such as the mirror, create an avant-garde and elegant atmosphere.

The combination of a normal white toilet with strong colors gives the space dynamism and a cheerful mood. If these colors are dark, it is useful to have a good light source.

The contrast between colors and lighting from above focusing on the toilet, boxed in a glass case, make it almost a domestic work of art.

The designers have succeeded in making the fixtures almost imperceptible in this minimalist bathroom with an attractive wood floor.

Even the most radical decorative options, those verging on kitsch, must have a unifying decorative element. In this case, the wooden toilet lid provides a note of simplicity in an over-elaborate environment.

Indoor swimming pools can be enjoyed throughout the year, whatever the outside temperature, but require specific care.

If possible, outdoor pools should be built in clear areas of the garden where there are no elements that create shade.

If there is not sufficient space to build a conventional pool, you can opt for one with an elongated shape like the one in the photo, with a minimum width of around 6 feet 6 inches (2 meters).

This is a truly spectacular pool. Its transparent glass wall allows you to see inside it. Furthermore, the unusual structure of the house makes the swimming pool appear to "hang" over a void as though it were a handrail attached to the terrace.

The parapet or low wall that surrounds this pool can be useful if, for example, you want to prevent children falling into the pool by accident.

Stone blocks acting like a bridge allow you to cross the lake-pool surrounding this house and connect the living room with the garden.

1 Three open skylights illuminate this pool midway between indoors and outdoors. A metal staircase connects the pool with the terrace.

2 Glass panels act as an almost invisible barrier for this pool, which seems to merge with the sea below.

3 Hanging plants have been placed on the beam positioned above this pool to give a sense of freshness.

4 If the pool is surrounded with trees and plants, you will need to regularly clean out the vegetation that falls in.

5 Round and oval pools are not recommended for small outdoor areas, because they waste useful space. Nevertheless, they are easier to clean than traditional rectangular pools.

6 Square or rectangular pools take advantage of the available land better, although they are harder to clean, particularly in the corners.

7 Wooden barriers and the climbing plants growing on them preserve the privacy of this small urban pool.

8 The inclined edges of this pool give it rather unconventional yet very attractive and innovative aesthetics.

9 The boundaries between pool, pond, and irrigation canal have completely disappeared in this case. A conventional pool would inevitably have broken the traditional aesthetics of the garden.

10 A platform has been built in the middle of this pond. The table and benches can be reached by crossing the stone blocks acting as a bridge.

The unusual triangular form of this pool allows maximum advantage to be gained from the shape of the terrain so as not to lose even a single square foot of useful space.

The unusual shape of this pool makes it seem to flow into the sea. The floor has been paved with stone, which dries quickly.

Elements

Once you have organized the distribution of space in your home—the location of the various rooms, access to them, and sources of light and ventilation—then you should go on to the next step, which is no less important, although less subject to fixed rules. Decorating and furnishing the home and deciding on accessories give it personality and make it a unique space. Selecting a style and choosing the atmosphere you want for your home will help you to keep on track and take the right decisions. The "right decisions" are those that help you to achieve the style you have chosen. A second option, which gives uncertain but undoubtedly surprising and definitely more contemporary results, is to opt for an eclectic style. Then your home gradually takes on a personality through the addition of objects, furniture, and unusual decorative elements, like a fruit that matures with the passing of time. The latter option is clearly more popular these days for many reasons, including the rising cost of buying property and the consequent reduction in size of urban houses, and the popularity of new types of family units and single lifestyles. Additionally, the Internet and new technologies enable you to easily acquire all manner of products, materials, and objects from any part of the world.

Once you have outlined your priorities and the distinctive features of your home (which may include not wanting to have any distinctive features), you can either get started or first conduct a small test. You could obtain small samples of the fabrics you have chosen and combine them on a sheet to see how they all fit together or put cut-out photos of the furniture on images of the various rooms of your home, to give you an idea of the final result. Whatever you do, it will offer you practical experience that will show you how to arrange the various elements of your home and how to decorate it. If you are too hasty and attempt to complete the furnishing and decorating work in just a few days, you are unlikely to achieve good results.

In contemporary interiors an excess of color can be a problem. Here the aim is to keep to a strict palette of black and white, with a black leather sofa and black and white cushions.

In minimalist interiors the items of furniture acquire a much greater significance than in more elaborate settings. The bench that joins the sofa to the large armchair has been upholstered with the same fabric to keep to the palette of colors in the design and avoid introducing a discordant element.

THE CURTAIN BOOK

ARCHITECTURE INTERIEURE
ET DECORATION EN FRANCE

In interiors with few striking decorative elements, it may be a good idea to use a printed fabric with cheerful patterns to cover the sofa and so make the room livelier without breaking the aesthetic mood chosen for it.

It is important for the upholstery chosen for the sofas and armchairs to match the carpet. A simple common color detail, such as the violet-colored flowers in this living room, will link the two elements visually.

There are hundreds of models of sofas on the market that allow you to arrange their various elements in any format you like. In this way, home-owners do not have to depend on a more or less standard configuration when decorating their dining room or living room.

An original cylindrical wooden armrest and a striking yellow color combine to make this sofa a decorative element with a strong personality.

7

8

1 Straight lines predominate in interiors in a Nordic style to create orderly and clean spaces. Obviously this desire for order also affects the sofas.

2 A sofa in a striking red color will quickly become the visual center of the room, so it makes sense to structure the decoration of the whole room around it.

3 For youthful and unorthodox interiors, it may be a good idea to opt for sofas with imaginative forms, strong colors, and up-to-date yet retro aesthetics.

4 Cushions on the floor help enclose the space defined by the sofa, the coffee table, and the carpet.

5 Sofas with a curved shape soften the harshness of interiors designed starting from clear straight lines. If they receive direct light from a window, they will also become one of the warmest corners in the house.

6 Sofas on wheels are an ideal solution for loft-type spaces, where it is usually convenient to have some movable elements that you can reorganize quickly and easily.

7 There are sofas on the market that can be adapted to practically any interior design, whether it has curved walls, different levels, minimal spaces, or a monochrome color scheme. This sofa fits perfectly against the curved wall behind it.

8 A sofa can divide a space in the same way as a partition or any other similar structural element.

9 Two relaxation areas located at either end of the same room should have sofas with very different aesthetics to avoid saturating the space.

10 The wood structure of this sofa combines perfectly with the original coffee table, also made of wood.

Light-colored furniture and upholstery create a calm, relaxed, and clear atmosphere. Uniform indirect top lighting is the most suitable here.

If there is a fireplace, the sofas should be positioned around it, since the home-owners will naturally be drawn to it as the focal point of the room.

Armchairs are one of the items of furniture that most define the personality of a room. One or two armchairs like those in the photo—white, rounded in shape, and with Pop Art aesthetics—give the space a very particular atmosphere.

Compact, sober armchairs with straight lines will be perceived visually as a block. They are therefore especially suited for minimalist interiors.

Some of the most famous armchairs in the history of design are still produced industrially by furniture manufacturers. They usually cost a lot more than common armchairs, but their visual weight is almost the same as a work of art.

There are hundreds of models of armchairs on the market, from the most classic to the most avant-garde, from the most sober to the most colorful, discreet or with a strong personality, antique or innovative. It is almost impossible not to find a model that fits the style of your home perfectly.

1 Armchairs that stand on a single leg are visually lighter. This is an advisable option if the armchair is accompanied by a footrest and you are afraid the group may be visually too heavy.

2 Armchairs can be upholstered in the same color as the sofa they accompany or they can contrast aesthetically with it, introducing a note of color into the space.

3 A simple armchair can become the visual center of the bedroom thanks to an intelligent use of colors.

4 Armchairs with wooden structures are both elegant and aesthetically flexible: they fit with virtually any decorative style.

5 Armchairs with tubular metal structures introduce an industrial note into warm surroundings.

6 The striking dark red armchair in the photo monopolizes the gaze of the casual observer, a sign of its powerful personality.

7 An armchair with an Expressionist shape can coexist perfectly with the most colorful and daring mixture of styles.

8 Combining two or three armchairs with radically different styles gives the room an unconventional and daring atmosphere, characteristic of a youthful space, particularly if one of them has been upholstered with a fabric imitating cowhide.

9 The imposing presence of the LC2 armchair designed by Swiss-French architect Le Corbusier becomes the visual center of any room.

10 The armchair in this room enjoys a wide space to "breathe," and does not have to compete visually with the rest of the furniture.

Tubular metal structures usually give armchairs a retro feel. It is not advisable to mix furniture that has a retro aesthetic with other contemporary items. If you are mixing styles, you should keep the visual personality of each element in mind and avoid overloading the atmosphere of the space.

These armchairs, which are shaped like balls truncated at the base and in their upper part, are direct heirs of the Bubble Chair by Finnish designer Eero Aarnio.

Armchairs in a Classical style, suitable for rooms decorated in a Baroque manner, are perfect for upholstering with floral print motifs. You can mix the upholstery and fabrics on the cushions and footrests.

The chairs with a curved structure in the photo have been chosen to balance the excessive coldness of the rest of the furniture and the pristine white floor and walls.

Chairs with open backs allow the body of the sitter to "breathe", so they are cooler than those with closed backs. Furthermore, panel backs are visually strong.

Classic chairs combine perfectly with contemporary furniture, although on account of their rarity, their personality will visually "absorb" the other decorative elements.

The presence of several chairs of the same model lined up under a long dining table gives the room a visual uniformity. In this example, their rounded forms soften the coldness created by having a number of the same object.

Two Hill House chairs, designed by Scottish architect Charles Rennie Mackintosh in the early 20th century, are enough to give personality to a space empty of any other decorative element.

Contemporary urban interiors require furniture that is functional, light, and comfortable, such as the set of chairs in this photo. They are not designed to last, but to be useful for a certain period of time and eventually to be replaced by others with a more up-to-date design.

1 The combination of wood and metal continues to be a popular preference for many designers of chairs; the results are almost always aesthetically perfect.

2 The Zig Zag chair by Dutch architect Gerrit Rietveld, designed in the 1930s, is based on minimal requirements, and its form remains as radical as when it was created. It is said that even the screws are decorative.

3 Original chairs from the 1960s and 1970s currently fetch very high prices, so people mostly opt for modern reproductions of the same quality. They are manufactured according to the original design but at far more affordable prices.

4 These original chairs with ethnic aesthetics produce an interesting effect in contrast with the coldness of the other elements in the room.

5 Some designs combine the Baroque style of the classic models with the materials and dynamism of new design, midway between two radically different aesthetic worlds.

6 A large table should have enough seats to surround its perimeter completely, otherwise the visual result will be poor.

7 Sober chairs with straight lines and classic materials are suitable for clear spaces where you want to project a sense of order.

8 If three or four different models of chairs are combined in the same space, try to ensure that they have something in common: the material (wood, for example), color, or a design belonging to the same decorative style.

9 Six chairs around a low table will form an "island," a distinct space separated from the adjoining area(s).

10 Purple, in its more bluish tones, transmits a sensation of depth. It is a daring color with a strong personality that does not fit in equally well with all decorative styles.

Chairs with straight lines and an avant-garde design run the risk of appearing cold. Therefore it makes sense to balance them with warm or colorful details. Otherwise the atmosphere becomes excessively industrial.

Details have a fundamental importance in Classical environments. Although an excess of elements may become Baroque, there is no need to be afraid of resorting to the use of cushions, tassels, and printed fabrics to "dress" a chair.

The furry seat balances the effect of the tubular steel structure of the chairs, which would otherwise be too cold for a Pop Art, youthful, and carelessly colorful interior.

Benches and stools are a fun alternative to more traditional chairs in the bedrooms of contemporary apartments.

Three stone benches together but arranged irregularly can easily turn into a table where, obviously, it is also possible to sit.

These benches with cushions are a perfect example of Scandinavian-style furniture; they are functional, elegant, and well suited for relaxed, simple settings.

Dark wooden furniture is particularly appropriate for interiors in a rustic style. The two cushions soften the hardness of the benches and give them warmth.

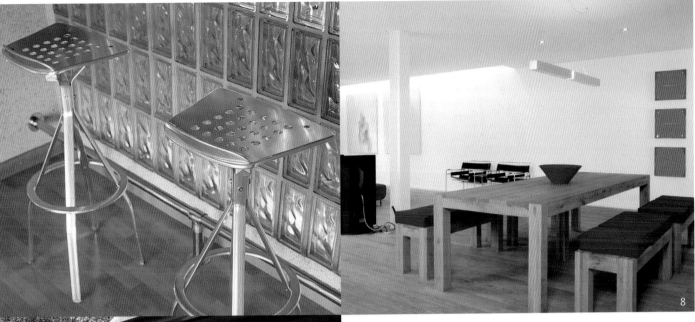

1 Sitting down at ground level with your legs inside a hollow cut into the floor is a habit in some Oriental cultures, which some people have adapted and reinterpreted for Western homes.

2 A bench upholstered with a fun fabric will introduce a touch of humor into the room.

3 Two benches positioned in parallel can be the perfect replacement for the more conventional sofa.

4 Stools are the appropriate accessory for modern kitchen islands, which in most cases are large enough to function as a working space and also as a dining table.

5 Colorful stools and pouffes function as an additional decorative element. There is a wide range of colors and different textures available for upholstering these items.

6 Original stools on wheels that can also act as small storage spaces (for magazines, for example) offer an alternative to traditional benches or chairs.

7 Metals are the most commonly used materials in furnishing contemporary kitchens on account of their modern aesthetics and high durability.

8 The red cushions on the benches around the table are replicated in the three decorative red squares on the wall.

9 Outdoor benches are a classic of urban landscaped spaces. They provide a place to rest outside.

10 Masonry benches, traditional in Mediterranean houses, are usually built both on terraces and in interiors.

A chair with adjustable height will allow you to work at tables of various heights without any problems. The chair back must be ergonomically shaped to avoid back problems.

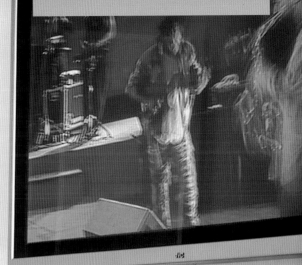

The rounded forms of these retro-inspired stools soften an interior style based on straight lines and a few decorative elements taken from a very limited palette of colors.

The Nordic style of decoration is very successful because its designers have been able to modernize traditional wooden furniture, particularly pale-colored items, giving them a contemporary air that is well suited to modern homes.

If you have a bar that separates the kitchen from the dining room or living room, it makes a good place to put some stools. In this way you gain an informal dining table.

Chairs with imaginative shapes using exotic materials are not hard to find nowadays in modern furniture stores. Their strong personality provides a striking decorative element in the home.

SKYSCRAPERS

The combination of a natural and warm material such as wood with a cold and industrial one such as aluminum can give good results in interiors with avant-garde or unconventional aesthetics.

The black footrests on these square stools give a striking note to the space and make it almost like a checkered Cubist painting.

A wooden block shaped like an hourglass can perform a dual function: it can act as a stool or a small table where you can place a vase, a flowerpot, or some other decorative element.

This compact table in the shape of an inverted U has enough space in its two legs to house several drawers. It is a robust furniture item and its presence will not go unnoticed.

This long table also functions as a banister for the stairway beside it. This is a way of taking advantage of a space that would not be properly exploited otherwise. The table is long enough for several people to work at it comfortably.

This is functionality and space saving taken to the extreme: the bench of this work table, almost a replica of the table it accompanies, fits perfectly under it.

Thanks to their spectacular design, some tables can practically function as decorative elements in their own right. This table has a reflective surface that attracts attention in the checkerboard-style room where it is located.

The combination of a natural material such as wood with a pure design (that is, a mixture of antique and modern) is suitable for homes where classic elements are combined with contemporary ones. In this case, the contrasting effect has been reinforced by leaving the coarse grain of the wood exposed.

This table with a very simple structure serves not only as a shelf or a side table for the TV, but also as a breakfast table—it can easily be slipped over the bed.

The metal slats that make up the backs and seats of the chairs for this dining table are replicated in the structure of the ceiling, which is also slatted. The structure of the table legs enables six chairs to be comfortably fitted under the table.

An original solution for a table with a purely decorative purpose: using two tubular columns as legs for a round metal table that is slightly inclined so as not to break the daring aesthetics of the rest of the house.

1 Tables placed in the center of the kitchen allow you to save space and avoid moving around the kitchen too much, as it is positioned much closer to the working area.

2 Tables that are oval or with rounded corners are less visually aggressive than those with sharp corners, although they also have a more marked personality with a greater impact on the decoration.

3 This table seems to float in space, thanks to an original (and almost invisible) anchoring system. The result is truly spectacular.

4 There are radical contrasts here: a kitchen with avant-garde, minimalist lines and a table with an irregular shape that imitates a slice of a tree trunk. The top has a reflective surface.

5 A table that is anchored at one end to the wall of the serving hatch allows you to save journeys from the kitchen to the dining room and vice versa.

6 The top of this multi-purpose table, which is supported at one of its ends by a bookcase, has had a section cut out so that the sofa fits into it. The table is the central axis of the room.

7 Tables on wheels are much easier to move than conventional ones. For this reason, they are ideal for youthful spaces or urban lofts, where the furniture is frequently reorganized.

8 White plastic tables are aesthetically innovative because they are so rare compared with more conventional tables made of wood or materials such as aluminum or glass.

9 Tables made of glass or transparent plastic visually lighten the space and are ideal for rooms with little natural lighting.

10 To give any space a minimalist atmosphere, there is nothing better than using cold materials and colors, such as white plastic.

If the top of the table is the same material and color as that chosen for the floor, the visual effect will be harmonious and elegant. This trick, which tends to make the table "blend in," is also used to visually lighten it if the table is too bulky.

In Spanish, a coffee table is called a *mesa de centro* (literally "center table") because it is positioned in the center of a space where the "walls" are generally sofas and armchairs. This space is usually considered as an independent area within the room.

Georges Braque

A table that breaks with the color scheme of the room, in this case blue in contrast with white and wood colors, stands out among the other furniture.

Coffee tables do not have to be low. In this case an original medium-height, circular-topped table with curved legs, similar to a bedside table, has been used as a coffee table.

This is an example of a purely decorative coffee table. It is left unadorned, since placing two items with strong personalities beside each other usually gives poor results.

A coffee table composed of four independent modules will allow you to modify the arrangement to increase or reduce the size of the table as required. It is a flexible and modern solution.

1 Tables with a single leg and a wide base are visually lighter than those with three or four legs.

2 The attractive turquoise color of this table combines perfectly with the chairs around it and with the photo of a beach landscape on the wall.

3 Two identical coffee tables allow you to divide the living room space in two, if you so wish. This is an ideal solution for large spaces and for when there are lots of visitors.

4 Some furniture breaks down the traditional boundary between tables and chairs; this item can function as a coffee table but also as a chair with contemporary aesthetics.

5 In minimalist spaces, the visual weight of the furniture is much greater than in conventional spaces. This makes it important to take great care in the choice of furniture: all the items must fit in and not jar with the group.

6 This coffee table, composed of three independent circular trays, gives dynamism and functions almost as if it were a small bookcase with shelves at different heights.

7 This unusual coffee table, composed of heavy blocks of wood, has undoubtedly become the visual center of the living room. The blocks can be moved around in any way you wish to change the shape of the table.

8 Two rectangular tables positioned in parallel form a square when together and can be repositioned depending on your needs.

9 A striking coffee table in the shape of an A on its side fits perfectly into the minimalist environment of this room.

10 This original coffee table is in perfect harmony with the sofas around it, thanks to the cushion placed on it, which also enables it to function as an auxiliary chair.

If you do not want to overload a room in a classic style, you should opt for a table with simple lines and neutral colors—these include white, black, and all the tones of gray and brown.

A coffee table on wheels is convenient and flexible. It also makes cleaning easier, although unstable objects should not be placed on it unless the wheels have a braking mechanism.

An 8-inch (20-cm) sill around the perimeter of the bed structure, next to the mattress, can function perfectly as a shelf for books, lamps, or other decorative elements. In practice it will become an additional bedside table.

The sides of the bed can reach down to the floor or stand a few inches above it. If you choose the former, you will not be able to keep any drawers under the bed, but the sides will give the bed a greater visual appearance.

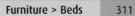

Many bed structures incorporate two or more drawers to store clothing, accessories, or other items. They are usually mounted on wheels and have the advantage that they make maximum use of the depth and width of the bed.

Placing the bed diagonally, with no other furniture beside it, makes the bed the central element of the room. This is a viable option if you choose a bed with a very unorthodox design like this one.

A bedside table on wheels can be moved as far from the bed or as close to it as you like. In some cases, as shown here, the bedside table can slide onto the bed frame to be used as a breakfast table.

The pillows and cover chosen for this bed give color to a monochrome bedroom. On a white background, any hint of color will take on more significance.

Combining different wood tones is an ever-popular option. The result is warm and gives the space a natural atmosphere, although it is a good idea to balance a possible excess of wood with items made of other materials, such as aluminum or glass.

1 In the case of rooms with a sloping wall, it is sensible to place the headboard of the bed at the lowest point of the wall to take maximum advantage of the height in the center of the room.

2 Three individual tatami mats used like a futon can be the base for a Western double bed mattress. It is advisable to air the tatami mats periodically by removing the mattress for a few hours.

3 The higher the legs of the bed, the easier it will be to clean underneath it.

4 The headboard of the bed does not always have to lean against a wall. Other perfectly practical types of arrangement exist.

5 A bed is not a purely functional piece of furniture. The bedclothes, the frame, and, above all, the headboard, can become excellent decorative elements, giving personality to the whole room.

6 Some headboards and bed structures allow you to fit small spotlights into them to replace the classic bedside table lamp.

7 A wide base will strengthen the personality of the double bed and make it much more striking.

8 A photo or painting in a large format over the headboard of the bed is one of the most typical decorative solutions in apartments in a contemporary style.

9 Beds with a canopy are usually chosen for traditional and Baroque-style bedrooms. They give a new dimension to the space and expand the decorative possibilities for the room in a spectacular fashion, enabling curtains, fabrics, and other ornamental elements to be hung from them.

10 A canopy with a contemporary design, straight lines, and manufactured in aluminum is an unorthodox and romantic alternative to a traditional bed.

This structure, similar to a canopy but just a few inches deep, allows you to surround the headboard area of the two single beds with a Provençale-style curtain.

The rough wooden structure of this double bed, similar to a pallet, is in strong contrast with the fabrics and pillows with floral motifs on the two large single mattresses. The effect is striking and original.

Light and semi-coarse fabrics have a perfect drop and are more decorative and natural than fabrics with a flat drop or fabrics that are excessively coarse or rigid. They are therefore ideal for modern canopies.

This is an avant-garde solution: a bed completely integrated with the rest of the furniture in the room, including the bathroom area. As it forms a block with the rest of the furniture, the visual result is practically futuristic.

Painting false moldings on the doors of the wardrobe is a fun and daring decorative option. In this case, the design is deliberately Naïve and is not intended to imitate a molding faithfully, but simply to add a colorful detail to the room.

Wardrobes fixed to the wall allow you to save space, although you need to check how solid the wall and the wall covering are before attaching such a heavy unit.

The lower wood strip introduces an element with strong decorative potential into a well-lit room.

There are two types of doors most commonly used in domestic wardrobes: conventional (leaf doors) and sliding doors. The former leave the interior of the wardrobe open to view but require space in front of them to be opened. The latter need less space but make the inside of the wardrobe less clearly visible.

The combination of two different types of doors, one positioned on the side, allows you to take maximum advantage of the capacity of this wardrobe.

An alternative to a traditional closed wardrobe is an open wardrobe. The one in the photo is a variant on the racks in clothes stores, where garments for sale are hung.

The greater the variety of units, drawers, and spaces in a wardrobe, the more you can make good use of it. If you carefully plan the distribution of space inside the wardrobe you can save space and gain storage capacity.

This wooden partition about 12 inches (30 cm) thick also functions as a wardrobe. It has folding doors to avoid the need to open the doors into the corridor.

The combination of closed wardrobes and open bookcases in the same unit is aesthetically perfect.

1 This striking wardrobe has shelves to hold small objects.

2 This wardrobe is in fact a bookcase that is concealed when its folding doors are closed.

3 Concealing the TV in a wardrobe may be a good idea if you do not want to have the set visible 24 hours a day.

4 The discreet presence of this built-in wardrobe leaves the limelight to the Hill House chair and to other decorative elements in the house.

5 A combination of closed and open units can be ideal if you want to have storage space as well as shelves for decorative items.

6 To enable you to make the best use of space, fitted wardrobes can be placed in practically any corner of the home. However, they are more expensive than free-standing ones.

7 A small wardrobe like this one can stand on a coffee table, in practice becoming an additional decorative element, similar to a vase.

8 The original translucent doors of this wardrobe lighten their visual weight, concealing their content slightly, but not completely.

9 Built-in wardrobes have minimal visual impact and allow you to take maximum advantage of the space available.

10 Here is an example of an open wardrobe: a bar hung from the cupboard above acts as a rail.

Glass doors allow you to see the contents of the wardrobe immediately while also protecting them from dirt and dust.

The elegance and strong personality of this wardrobe lie in the type of wood and the door handles.

If you want to disguise the presence of a wardrobe, the best option is to paint it the same color as the wall or the floor.

The original curved doors of this wardrobe combine perfectly with the undulating forms of the mirror to its left and give the decoration an organic touch.

The deep square drawers enable the capacity of the wardrobe to be exploited to the maximum because they can hold larger items than a conventional drawer.

Bookcases or shelves with backs are safer and more stable than those without them, although they are visually heavier and have a greater impact on the decoration of the space.

A fitted bookcase system can be adapted to suit any corner of the room. Access to the upper shelves can be gained using a library-style sliding ladder.

Bookshelves built into recesses in the walls allow you to save space. Painting them the same color as the wall into which they are built will concentrate the visual attention on the books or items you place on them.

The thickness and length of the shelves will depend on how much weight you wish to place on them: the heavier the weight, the thicker and shorter the shelf should be.

Shelves made of masonry or materials such as plasterboard give you extra storage space in small corners that are hard to access.

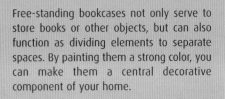

Free-standing bookcases not only serve to store books or other objects, but can also function as dividing elements to separate spaces. By painting them a strong color, you can make them a central decorative component of your home.

1 To have an idea of the length of shelving that you will need, you should usually multiply the approximate number of books you want to place on them by their average thickness. It is a good idea to add a few more feet of shelving, since the number of books tends to increase rather than decrease.

2 Classic wooden bookshelves are very elegant and visually powerful, although they are not very flexible and adaptable. They are more decorative than practical.

3 Decorative elements will stand out much more if you place them on a shelf beneath a window or a skylight that illuminates them properly.

4 Masonry shelves are typical of Mediterranean houses. They usually have an almost exclusively decorative function, although their robustness makes them appropriate to house heavy objects.

5 The minimum thickness of a shelf that will support the weight of books must be between 1 and 1.2 inches (2.5 and 3 cm).

6 Shelves should be lit uniformly, avoiding any dark areas, so you can locate what you are looking for quickly.

7 If you want to place a lamp on a bookshelf, try to position it on one of the lower shelves, which usually receive less natural light.

8 The dead space below a staircase is the ideal corner to place a fitted bookcase; you can make it whatever depth you want, although more than 16 inches (40 cm) is usually not practical.

9 The small recess in this furniture item that acts as a partition has some visually very light glass shelves installed in it.

10 The unused space that remained between the upper part of the wardrobe and the ceiling has been used to install shelving made of cubic modules.

The combination of plastic seats and a wooden table transfers the traditional dichotomy between the antique and the modern, typical of contemporary interiors, to the terrace of this home.

Two original beach chairs made of wooden slats contrast radically with the facade of metal sheets on this house with avant-garde aesthetics.

In this small apartment a wooden bench has been built between the attractive green wall and the handrail. Some cushions cover the bench and make it a genuine outdoor sofa.

This is an exercise in radical contrast: a terrace with rustic aesthetics paved with wooden boards and a table and chairs in Pop Art style, manufactured in white methacrylate and aluminum.

A barrier of cane fencing conceals the terrace of this urban apartment from the neighbors' sight. The plants give the space warmth, and the flowerpots become another decorative element.

Iron and tropical wood are two of the most appropriate materials for outdoor furniture, thanks to their high resistance to humidity and bad weather.

Four armchairs with their corresponding footrests and two rocking-chairs are all the furniture needed to create an idyllic and relaxing space to rest under the porch of this two-storey house.

A combination of bench and chairs will be more flexible than opting exclusively for a pair of benches or half a dozen chairs.

1 Wicker furniture is another classic on terraces. Its aesthetics are warm and welcoming.

2 Two simple outdoor seats and a low table can be sufficient to create, from very little, an inviting corner to rest and relax.

3 Installing a sofa outside under the balcony of the upper floor of the house will protect you from the sun's rays.

4 This outdoor fireplace enables everyone to gather around it when the temperatures are not as warm as you would like. A coffee table, a pair of armchairs, and a sofa complete an inviting meeting space.

5 Combining small flowerpots with other larger ones will brighten up your terrace and avoid the sensation of being in a prefabricated space.

6 The unusual structure of this terrace, an updating of the traditional Roman atrium, allows you to install a hammock.

7 The original canopies over the wicker benches on this terrace give them a romantic and decidedly bohemian air. The silky drop of the fabric contributes to this effect.

8 Here is an original alternative to typical wooden outdoor tables: a large table (or two together) made of aluminum.

9 Plants are the main feature of this terrace with a sea view. When you have a beautiful natural environment such as this, it is best not to overload the space with other elements.

10 Some removable cushions can transform a simple step into a large outdoor sofa.

Teak is one of the materials most used for outdoor furniture. Its dark color and elegant texture are two of its strong points.

Coarse and natural, fine woven and elegant, there are hundreds of different kinds of carpets on the market. As a general rule, a carpet gives personality to a space and can serve to separate different areas of the same room.

A carpet in various shades of purple and a yellow sofa with orange cushions give color to a space decorated in neutral tones using natural materials.

In a space where you are not seeking harmony but radical contrast, a carpet can easily become a key decorative element. In this case, the red, white, and black colors of the carpet break with the tones of the plastic panels of the partition in the background.

Colorful carpets with ethnic motifs are ideal for spaces with a bohemian atmosphere. In this case, the carpet has become a visual replica of the books in the bookcase in the background.

7

8

9

10

1 Carpets with rather unusual shapes, such as the heart shape here, are appropriate for youthful, unconventional spaces.

2 Upholstery with fringes and carpets with floral motifs, generally brightly colored, are appropriate for classic interiors, in Provençale or English style.

3 Two colored cushions on the carpet give the space warmth and magically turn it into a meeting space.

4 In this case the carpet, which is the same color as the chairs, table, and sofa, gives the space continuity and visual rhythm.

5 The decorative edging of a carpet reinforces its presence and defines the space even more strikingly, eliminating any sensation of visual continuity between the carpet and the floor.

6 The three small rugs in this classic living room function as visual guides, marking the various areas into which the space is divided. The central rug marks both the boundary between two spaces and the "corridor" for entering and leaving the room.

7 Furry carpets are appropriate for contemporary spaces to which you want to give an irreverent and youthful touch.

8 Uneven materials such as raffia or coconut fiber are less flexible than other types of fabric, although they are also more resistant. They will give contemporary environments a note of dynamism.

9 Depending on the owner's tastes, carpets can become harmonious or discordant elements. In this case a contrast has been chosen between the coarse aesthetics of the floor and wall coverings and the coloring of the carpet.

10 Carpets are one of the most useful elements if you want to mix styles, thanks to their wide variety of colors, patterns, forms, and materials.

CUSHIONS

Cushions are one of the warmest decorative elements you can use. A few cushions of different colors and sizes will always be welcoming and invite rest and relaxation.

Typical Indonesian cushions, generally consisting of six cylinders sewn together, are increasingly popular in modern interiors.

Cushions on the floor may offer a good alternative to traditional armchairs. They are more discreet and much more flexible. If they are not required, they can quickly be put away somewhere else.

In this house decorated with a palette of neutral colors, bright colors have been reserved for the cushions, which introduce a warm counterpoint to the coldness of the room.

Cushions are differentiated not only by their color or patterns but also by their fabrics, finishes, forms, and textures.

The thicker the fabric of the cushion, the greater the sensation of robustness. Cotton fabrics are the most common, although velvet and linen are also very popular.

Cushions are easier to wash if the padding and covers are independent, and the latter can be removed easily.

The fun knots of this cushion introduce an organic contrast into a living room with pure lines and a rather sterile atmosphere.

1 Cushions with different prints give an unconventional note of color to this loft with an industrial appearance. The original floor needed to be combined with some kind of element to lighten the space.

2 Ethnic-style prints and embroidery have become extraordinarily popular in recent years. They are usually found in homes with a modern and bohemian style, although they are appropriate for practically any contemporary style.

3 The small cushions in this photo act as decorative elements owing to their small size. They resemble candies spread over the three benches on wheels in the center of the room.

4 The combination of various tones of the same color, in this case brown, helps the cushions to create a truly welcoming atmosphere.

5 Cushions with intense colors are recommended to liven up the appearance of armchairs with white or neutral upholstery.

6 Before opting for a fabric with special characteristics like the one in the photo, you should evaluate very carefully whether it will fit the decorative style you seek for your home.

7 Combining cushions with different fabrics and colors may be a good way to visually liven up a room that is too serious.

8 Placing two or more overlapping cushions on a very deep sofa allows you to create many different combinations as well as play with color and textures.

9 A few cushions are all that is needed to quickly create a relaxing rest area for tea in the garden.

10 Placing the same combination of different cushions at each end of a sofa gives it a truly attractive symmetry.

Two mirrors positioned symmetrically on a shelf become decorative elements similar to a painting. The color of the frames is the same as that of the walls, giving the space a sensation of visual continuity.

1 A mirror can work exactly the same way as a sculpture or a painting. In some cases, it can have an even greater effect.

2 Mirrors in bathrooms help visually enlarge these spaces, which are frequently small.

3 Mirrors installed near the bathtub increase the sensation of space, but they require continuous maintenance to avoid the buildup of limescale.

4 A mirror placed over a checkered surface that reflects a wall covered in the same way creates a playful and amusing visual effect.

5 In addition to their obvious practical purpose, mirrors are excellent decorative elements. They also give the space a sensation of spaciousness and brightness.

6 A spectacular mosaic of mirrors of various sizes and shapes transforms this bathroom into a genuine work of art. The floor has been paved in the same way to maintain the decorative rhythm.

7 This is an original option: a mirror in the form of a waning moon embracing a circular window. Beside it is the small mirror that has "broken off" from the large one.

8 Some mirrors can be considered as full-blown works of art, so they fulfill a double function.

9 Rectangular mirrors hung vertically increase the visual height of the room. When hung horizontally, they will make it look longer.

10 A wooden frame with carved moldings is ideal for interiors with a rustic or Provençale inspiration.

Mirrors enlarge the space where they are hung, although this effect is reduced if the mirror has a frame. The wider the frame, the less the sensation of spaciousness that the mirror will provide.

Mirrors function as decorative elements: they can be painted or etched, among many other finishes and techniques, to achieve any effect you desire.

Some very wide and striking mirrors provide a fun detail to this Nordic-style bathroom.

Mirrors fitted over the washbasin in a
bathroom must be lit uniformly to avoid
areas of shade falling on the viewer's face.

A mirror placed on the outer wall of a bathtub will make the floor opposite it appear larger, so it is an original and suitable solution for small spaces.

A small mirror with an adjustable arm and a magnifying glass effect, suitable for precision tasks, has been added to the large mirror in this bathroom.

A mirror fitted on one of the doors of the bathroom closet will reduce its visual weight and lighten the space.

Natural details give warmth to interior spaces. In this case, a small pool with some fish replaces a conventional fish tank.

This industrial shed converted into a loft has a space in the center with a rectangle just 6 feet x 9 feet (6 meters square) where a palm tree is growing, along with an indoor species in a pot.

1 Some very tall indoor potted plants have been placed behind the translucent blue glass panel fitted into the headboard of this bed. The effect is extraordinarily striking.

2 Vine arbors protect from the sun and at the same time help maintain the privacy of the house. They are increasingly common on urban terraces.

3 Some species of indoor plants, move naturally found in warm climates, can adapt to the interior of a home if they have the necessary light and heat to grow.

4 Pots of all shapes, colors, and sizes are easy to find today, with designs to suit any decorative style.

5 An elegant option is to plant flowers of the same color in flowerpots on the terrace, to achieve a two-color combination with a detail of a different color.

6 These canes create an attractive feature. They appear to sprout from the floor of the bathroom and combine perfectly with the color scheme of the room.

7 A small vase can make an excellent decorative element. Having a group of vases is visually spectacular.

8 Bathrooms tend to be cold spaces that should be balanced using warm decorative items, such as paintings, plants, or objects with no function other than being purely decorative.

9 The lush vegetation on this terrace makes it a small urban oasis, a piece of countryside in the city.

10 To give warmth to a room designed in cool tones, it may be a good idea to place a few flowers in vases of the same color as the walls or the other decorative elements.

In a home surrounded by vegetation, plants will fulfill the function of integrating the exterior and interior spaces.

Two simple leaves in two unusual white vases are the only color detail in this elegant home that uses neutral tones and traditional materials.

A small pool where some water lilies are floating, as in the photo, will eliminate the boundary between the interior and exterior of the house, giving the room a sophisticated Zen air of relaxation.

An artistic work like this, consisting of stones of various textures and sizes and a composition of dry branches on a wooden block, will give warmth and easily become a focus of attention in the room.

An aluminum jug painted white with flowers, like the one in the photo, is a decorative detail that is quickly associated with homes in a rustic or country style.

On occasions, a simple flower in a vase with a contemporary design is much more striking than a more spectacular bunch of flowers. The secret lies in knowing how to play with the contrasts of colors and forms.

1 A fish tank has been built into the wall that separates the dining room from the other rooms of this house. In this way it becomes a "living painting."

2 A group of five or six small pots with flowers of various colors gives visual rhythm and a likable detail to the dining room window.

3 This is an original way of utilizing a "dead" corner in the structure of the home. It has been transformed into a small garden, opened to the interior through glass doors.

4 The colorful mixture of aquatic plants and bushes on this terrace is its main attraction. The flowers give color and balance where there would otherwise be an excess of green tones.

5 The bunch of flowers in the center of the dining table is replicated in the bunch in the background of the photo, providing a sense of balance.

6 In this case the personality of the "green" room of the house has been enhanced by means of a soft floor covering that imitates a lawn. The result is original and provocative.

7 A simple flower dramatically breaks up the Pop Art decoration of this dining room, demonstrating that a simple detail can sometimes have a more dynamic effect than huge furniture items.

8 Combining vases of different shapes, colors, and sizes with flowers of various colors gives the room dynamism and turns it into a "living" space.

9 The warm yellow tones of this house are replicated in the tulips of the same color that dominate the coffee table in the living room.

10 Rooms with a very cold feel can be counterbalanced by a simple group of vases; in these, grass has been planted.

Overhanging fireplaces have a base that is not at floor level, but a certain distance above it. Here, although the fireplace is not in contact with the floor, the area around it has been covered with a fireproof material.

When a fireplace has been installed in the center of the room, it acquires a much greater decorative significance. The various elements of the room must therefore be organized around it.

1 In living rooms with fireplaces, the distribution of the furniture is usually organized in a U shape around it, without a coffee table.

2 Some fireplaces have a space beside them that allows you to store the firewood. The wooden mantelpiece of the fireplace therefore becomes a decorative feature where you can place ornamental objects.

3 You can place decorative elements on a glass mantelshelf over the fireplace to attenuate the hardness of the metal structure of the fireplace itself.

4 The fireplace in the photo has a dual personality: it is striking on one hand but minimalist on the other. Depending on the decoration around it, it could take on either characteristic.

5 The fireplaces in classic-style houses have jambs and trims that are richly ornamented with moldings and engravings of foliage.

6 A closed, purely decorative fireplace can also be a valid alternative for interiors in a contemporary style.

7 Many modern fireplaces have prefabricated metal tubes that act as ducts to eliminate smoke. They are usually left visible as a decorative element.

8 The open window to the right of the fireplace acts as a counterpoint and gives harmony to the arrangement, preventing the attention from being too focused on the lower part of the wall.

9 This original overhanging fireplace has completely concealed the flue of the fireplace, integrating it masterfully into the wall that supports it.

10 This original fireplace, displayed in a showcase and similar to a fish tank, gives the room an unusual personality.

A spectacular stone wall accommodates a built-in fireplace constructed on a sill about 12 inches (30 cm) above floor level. The mantelshelf is a wooden beam that the owners of the house wanted to conserve and is here used to striking effect.

Integrating a fireplace elegantly into a space decorated in a classic style is not always easy. Painting the jambs and mantelpiece of the fireplace the same color as the wall helps integrate it smoothly.

A metal guard covers this fireplace, which stands on a stone hearth to prevent any sparks flying onto the wood floor of the room.

Color and light

The combination of good natural lighting and a successful use of colors usually gives a home a warm and pleasant atmosphere. Clearly, the best light is natural, although you will inevitably need several sources of artificial lighting, either general or direct, to light the dark areas of your home. In any case, the basic rule is to place as few items as possible in front of sources of natural light so that it can spread into all the corners. Natural light, much warmer than artificial light, makes the colors of the walls, floors, and furniture adopt various tones, and therefore suggests differing moods as the day goes on. In general, pale tones, and particularly white, will reflect light and make the home seem larger than it actually is. Dark tones absorb light and make the room appear smaller, although the final result will depend on the combination of tones chosen (a room with black slate floors and white walls gives a different result from the reverse). If you can master the various combinations of tones and brightness, your home will have a different atmosphere depending on your needs or your mood.

Just as color contrasts usually give good results and make a room cheerful, sudden contrasts in light intensity are almost always annoying. Although it is obvious that the working area, the kitchen, or the bathroom should have more powerful lighting than is needed in other spaces in the home, it is advisable to soften the transitions so that your eyes are not constantly forced to refocus and adapt to these different levels, which may even cause headaches. As for colors, each one is generally associated with a different mood, and opting for some at the expense of others will depend entirely on your preferences. In general, neutral colors, mainly white, are best when you are attempting to create a "canvas" on which to place brightly colored objects that you wish to highlight. In contrast, striking colors on floors and walls tend to blend in with the objects placed on them, unless the contrast is extraordinarily abrupt—a black vase on a shelf on a red wall, for example.

Color

Light

Yellows, reds, and oranges are warm colors. They give a sensation of warmth and bring to mind the sun's rays.

The color red and its derivatives absorb light and are therefore not very appropriate for poorly lit spaces, although they give the interior design vitality and forcefulness.

The intensity of the red sliding panels is replicated in the yellow upholstery and the orange cushions of the sofa located opposite them, giving balance to the room.

7

8

9

0

1 Natural light will yellow any surface that it hits, although it will obviously have a greater effect if the surface is a warm color.

2 Warm colors produce the visual sensation of "advancing" in the observer if they are used on large surface areas. Cool colors, on the other hand, produce the opposite effect.

3 The warm orange color of this room balances the greenish, cooler tone of the adjacent room.

4 Pink is the dominant color chosen for this room with a youthful atmosphere. The neutral tone of the wall and the white of the floor tone down the warmth of the pink and lilac.

5 A red carpet gives warmth and vigor to a room where neutral colors are prevalent.

6 The warmth of the orange seats in the dining room and the painting in the photo combine perfectly with interiors that are predominantly white.

7 Combinations of violet and purple usually give good results if they are placed over "canvases" that are white or of warm colors.

8 Painting the ceiling red and the walls white will make the former seem higher. The other way round, the opposite effect is achieved.

9 Very large rooms appear cold, so it is a good idea to paint them with warm colors such as yellow to make them welcoming.

10 Warm colors in the bathroom avoid the uncomfortable sensation of coldness that is caused by greenish or bluish colors.

The warm tones of this photo of an autumn landscape balance the coldness of the aluminum furniture in front of it.

The texture of surfaces and covering affects our perception of color. Smooth textures reflect light while rough ones absorb it.

The color yellow is associated with the sun's rays. It has an arousing effect and is said to stimulate the intelligence. It is the most luminous of the warm colors.

Decorating the paneling on a wall with stripes is a radical and daring decorative move. Painting the upper part of the wall an analogous color to that of the stripes will tone down and balance the final result.

Yellow combines perfectly with blue because it is very close to orange, the complementary color to blue on the color wheel. This is a classic combination.

Cool colors (greens, blues, and violets) give the spectator the sensation of distance with respect to the object. This is why they are generally used in spaces you wish to enlarge visually.

Yellow with a greenish tinge is also considered a cool color. The darker the tone of a cool color, the cooler it will be. It occasionally requires contrasts in the form of details in warm colors or natural materials like wood.

Cool colors in their paler tones are slightly warmer than in their dark tones. All of them transmit a sense of calm, so they are ideal for bedrooms, for example.

Vertical lines will make the space seem higher than it actually is. If the lines are a cool color, the effect will be doubled.

Cool colors are also very often used by interior designers in bathrooms because of the sense of calm and serenity they transmit.

Monochrome options are a safe bet, even when you choose to combine two or three tones of the same color. Natural light will in itself create different hues of color with the passing hours of the day.

To give dynamism to cool monochrome color schemes, it is advisable to use different materials and textures. Silk or linen curtains, velvet fabrics to upholster the chairs, cotton rugs and, of course, wood for the floor and some furniture items will be sufficient to attenuate the monochrome effect.

Cool tones are not necessarily as boring as they may appear at first sight. A simple detail in a lighter color (a cream-colored closet, in this case) provides a contrast and makes the space more dynamic.

The electric blue used to paint the walls of this bedroom has its coolness both counterbalanced and enhanced: the white bedclothes and the wood tend to neutralize it, while the purple blanket accentuates it.

Blue is a relaxing color, which is why it is used in bathrooms. In its paler tones, that is to say, those containing more white, it is much less cool than in its dark tones. In this case, the white wood beams also soften its coolness.

The difference in tone that can be observed between the door in the background and the staircase in the foreground illustrates the differences that natural light (and also artificial light) make to the same color.

1

2

3

4

5

　Color and light

6

1 The coolness of blue tones is reinforced by the presence of materials such as aluminum, glass, or plastic.

2 The darker tones of wood can become cool if they are surrounded by neutral colors such as black or white.

3 Blue tones transmit calm and serenity, so they are ideal for spaces with a Zen inspiration or to be used as chill-out zones.

4 The color green in any of its tones—but particularly those closest to yellow—in combination with white gives the room a sensation of freshness.

5 If the space is correctly lit, a partition in a very cool color, such as the dark violet in the photo, can combine very well with the prevalence of white. This is a way of breaking up the environment visually in bathrooms with an austere appearance.

6 The chrome and reflective surfaces typical of contemporary kitchens accentuate the sensation of coolness of some colors, so they are usually balanced by means of strong lighting.

7 Cooler orange tones are recommended for refreshing predominantly white interiors where you want to accentuate a Pop Art atmosphere.

8 Neutral colors such as gray, black, and white act as a perfect frame for cool tones.

9 A well-considered combination of warm and cool colors gives the space an ideal balance and creates an atmosphere that is relaxing but not boring.

10 Neutral whitish and grayish tones are particularly appreciated in minimalist interiors, thanks to their discreet and very non-aggressive personality.

A palette of neutral colors considerably enhances decorative details or furniture with warm colors, especially red. Artificial materials such as plastic will emphasize this contrast, perhaps in the most radical way.

Blue and purple, two cool colors, form one of the classic combinations in interiors with a bohemian atmosphere. Using the same color for the ceiling and the walls intensifies the perception of blue as a cool color.

A palette of cool and warm colors fits perfectly in youthful interiors. Blue favors study and concentration, while red and orange tones stimulate and enliven the decoration.

Another classic combination of a cool and a warm color: blue and yellow. In this case the warm one has been reserved for the large surfaces (the walls) and the cool one for the small ones (the window frame). This is the safest option.

A warm color like yellow will tend to be perceived as cool in rooms that are poorly lit, and even more so if it has been used to cover walls made of cold materials such as stone or concrete.

A space painted white is brighter than one painted in dark colors. The thermal sensation is also different—cool for the former, warm for the latter.

Traditional lampshades in the form of truncated cones project light up and down, leaving an area poorly lit in between, which can be used to produce various lighting effects if you play with several lamps.

Spaces that have a good source of natural light can be painted or have their floors covered with dark colors, although it is advisable to supplement the lighting with some points of artificial light.

Glass walls and pale colors are ideal for small spaces or for homes where you want to take maximum advantage of the little existing natural light.

The tiles used to cover the bathroom surfaces may be exactly the same or in various tones of the same color. In the latter case, the light will be reflected on them differently, causing dynamic visual effects.

Canvas roller blinds allow you to tone down and regulate the light entering the room through the windows. In this case, the aim was to diffuse the light by choosing a color tone for the blinds in the same range as the upholstery of the sofas.

Monochrome interiors do not have to be boring if you make use of different tones of the same color and the variations of light in the room.

Narrow windows at the top of the walls are not a sufficiently abundant light source to allow the walls of this room to be covered with a dark color. Light wood is the most suitable choice in this case.

Dark brick walls absorb the light, so they are only advisable in spaces with good natural lighting. The glass block wall allows light to enter from the adjoining room.

Monochrome interiors give a space the sensation of continuity. The high ceilings and abundant natural light of this house have made it possible to paint the wooden ceiling black, a choice that is not always advisable.

1 Radical decorative options, such as creating a room where all the elements are white, may be visually spectacular, although it will considerably limit your freedom when you decorate and light the space.

2 Lamps are not only functional elements; their style and personality affect to a large degree the color and brightness of the room, enhancing or toning down the other elements.

3 Lamps with daring and radical designs give the space vitality and vigor, depending on the tone and scope of the light they emit.

4 The partition positioned in front of the window helps diffuse a whitish light over the space to its right and left, although it leaves the area behind it in half-light.

5 The floor lamp provides a good level of light around it, the so-called "cloak of light," while the function of the candles is decorative, in this case associated with the pastel tones of the room. The candles do not contribute to the lighting.

6 Human beings receive 80% of the information on their environment through vision, hence the need for adequate lighting. Pale decoration in the room makes it easier to light.

7 The overhanging steps of this room create imaginative and attractive interplays of light and shade beneath them, thanks to the light they receive through the skylight above.

8 Building lights into the ceiling is harder than hanging a simple lamp from it, but it is an appropriate option for minimalist spaces such as this monochrome living room.

9 Powerful but perfectly diffused lighting will convert a white kitchen into a space of immaculate purity.

10 The workspace of the kitchen should always be lit with plenty of lights, particularly if the furniture is dark in color.

To enable the natural light that enters through the windows to reach all possible corners of the room, you should avoid placing large opaque furniture items in front of them.

In eclectic-inspired or radically kitsch spaces, you can give free rein to your imagination by opting for discordant tones and lamps with totally disparate styles and degrees of brightness.

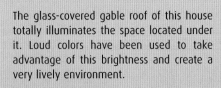

The glass-covered gable roof of this house totally illuminates the space located under it. Loud colors have been used to take advantage of this brightness and create a very lively environment.

This colorful Pop Art-inspired interior design is sprinkled with dozens of small decorative details. A variety of tones are combined, and the space is saturated with an explosion of colorful details, such as the chair backs, the back wall, and the ceiling.

The abundant colors in this bedroom benefit from the profusion of natural light that enters through the door. The yellow wall acts as a canvas on which paintings and decorative objects in a huge variety of colors are arranged.

Impastoed (highly pigmented) colors, which have a large quantity of black, are mainly suitable for very well-lit spaces. It is a good idea to combine them with tones that are distant on the color wheel, as in this living room, to brighten up the space.

This interior is an example of how different tones should be combined within a pastel range and how the same color appears differently depending on how it is lit—as demonstrated in the two adjacent rooms.

Spotlights built into the ceiling and floor allow you to free up space, avoiding the proliferation of ceiling and wall lamps. The small candles create drama and theatricality and have a purely decorative purpose.

Floor lamps, very commonly used in the 1960s and 1970s, have fallen out of favor, except in Pop Art-inspired interiors. Their main advantage, leaving aside the purely aesthetic aspect, is that they illuminate areas far from their bases.

An aluminum tube holds several spotlights that can easily be adjusted to light areas very far away from each other.

Inbuilt or surface-mounted spotlights are sometimes left visible, including their cables, making them an additional decorative element.

A spectacular and striking chandelier houses various candles to give drama to the classic- and rustic-inspired interior design of this house.

Lamps do not have a purely utilitarian function, but can also serve as excellent decorative elements. The bedside table lamp in the photo humorously imitates the shape of a bulb.

Any decorative element with strong colors that you place against a black background will stand out clearly, claiming all the visual attention in the room—like this orange lamp.

1 Two floor lamps placed side by side illuminate in the same way as a single more powerful one and have a much greater aesthetic and decorative impact.

2 You can use additional lighting to highlight decorative elements and focus attention on them or to create a certain atmosphere.

3 Candles illuminate the space where they are used very weakly, so they are basically used for decorative purposes or as atmospheric lighting.

4 Two spotlights built into the ceiling light the painting on the wall to concentrate attention on it. This is the most common option when strong direct lighting is required.

5 For spaces with industrial aesthetics, it may be a good—and original—idea to use powerful spotlights as used by photography or movie professionals.

6 A red lampshade against a white background attracts the spectator's gaze. It will become the central element in the room where it is used, provided there is no other item competing with it.

7 The two floor lamps illuminate the dining room table with a warm, uniform light, which is ideal for the white and greenish tones chosen for the walls and main furniture items in the room.

8 If you do not need excessive brightness and you prefer to give a space a calm and relaxed atmosphere, then you can use lamps that produce a light with warm and diffused tones.

9 Any logo, photo, or design printed on a lampshade will really attract attention. In this case, the lamp acts like a light box.

10 Direct lighting can be used to highlight a single decorative object, such as a painting.

A powerful design light illuminates the stairway leading to the lower floor and the space above it. This light is strong, but concentrated on specific points in the space.

Height-adjustable pendant spotlights can be positioned at various heights as required, although if used this way, their light beam cannot be directed toward any point other than the floor.

In Mediterranean houses it is common to find terraces illuminated by candlelight alone. Artificial lighting would spoil the atmosphere.

Lighting is one of the sectors where new trends in design have arrived with a vengeance. There are models and designs for all decorative styles, from the most classic to the most radically avant-garde.

Choosing wall lamps and lamps with radically contrasting aesthetics will give the space dynamism. Here, the abundant natural light has made it possible to play with lamps with a more decorative than purely functional purpose.

Where possible, lamps and wall lamps should complement the natural light rather than replacing it.

Lights that are colored or toned down by some translucent element, such as this screen, provide a luminosity that is not very powerful but is greatly decorative, with strong contrasts.

7

8

9

10

1 Sources of indirect lighting and built-in spotlights are generally comfortable to the eyes. They are unlikely to cause dazzling or discomfort.

2 Light rails not only allow you to alter the direction of the spotlights, in most cases, but also to increase or reduce their number depending on your needs.

3 Translucent plastic walls or screens allow the light to pass through and easily become decorative elements in their own right. In this case, the bathroom acts as a light box.

4 Lamps composed of a number of spotlights are very versatile and allow you to switch on just some of them or direct the light beam from each spotlight to a different point of the room, according to your requirements.

5 Some light sources not only have a functional purpose but also sometimes act as key decorative elements. The small lights in the ceiling of this house, each with between one and ten watts of power, appear like a starry sky.

6 Spotlights built into the floor help you create imaginative effects of light and color with the least possible aesthetic impact.

7 Adapting your pupils to the light in a room, in the same way as the diaphragm of a camera, is always easier when the sources produce a uniform light or are indirect, as in the case of cornice lighting.

8 In outdoor spaces it is usual to combine localized lighting, such as in the entrance porch, with direct lighting on an object or a very specific point.

9 Cavetto lighting has been chosen in this corridor, although in this case the light source is not concealed behind a molding but behind the partition itself. The pink tone of the light emitted by those spotlights provides an unorthodox detail to the interior design of the house.

10 Indirect lighting is the most appropriate for areas where you do not need a high level of brightness concentrated on a specific point or a small area.

The inappropriate use of a number of light sources may be visually overwhelming, so it is preferable to repeat some element rhythmically—in this case, the candle-like wall lamps.

As far as possible, bookcases should be lit uniformly to prevent the upper shelves being less well lit than the lower ones (or vice versa), which would force you to adjust your pupils too quickly.

Reading areas should be lit sufficiently so you do not have to strain your sight at all.

The four lamps lighting the bar hang from flexible cables. The height can be adjusted as required by means of a counterbalance.

The lights over the kitchen work area should illuminate the area uniformly to avoid dark areas.

A light rail runs along the entire length of the kitchen, which is like a corridor in this house. The yellowish tones of the light give warmth to a room where very cool greenish tones predominate.

7

8

9

10

1 The flexible cables on which the pendant lamps hang can also become attractive decorative elements.

2 Circular lights act as visual foci in the home. They instinctively attract people's gaze, functioning as powerful decorative elements.

3 Lamps that produce colored lights are tremendously decorative, but you must keep in mind that they will have a significant effect on the decoration of the space.

4 Skylights allow you to take advantage of the natural light that the house receives through the roof. They are normally used in rooms where, for whatever reason, it is impossible to have windows or these are insufficient to light the space properly.

5 The lamp with a shade in the shape of a truncated cone in this dining room provides a good level of general light, while the directional spotlights in the ceiling project their light toward the particular areas that require lighting.

6 On this type of terrace it is common to opt for lamps with an ethnic inspiration that emit a purely decorative or atmospheric light.

7 The perimeter of this urban balcony has been highlighted by means of low-voltage lights hidden under the handrail, which make it appear to "float" above the ground.

8 In a room with pure lines and few decorative elements with organic forms, you can observe in great detail the light effects achieved by the indirect light sources.

9 In this home an exquisite contrast has been achieved between the natural light source (the windows) and artificial sources of general lighting, localized and direct. High ceilings allow you to play with the different intensities and tones of the light much more effectively.

10 Five spotlights built into the false ceiling, aligned on one side of the room rather than in the center, are enough to illuminate these narrow spaces effectively.

A platform suspended from the ceiling houses dozens of candles that provide a warm and welcoming light for the dining room of this house with large windows.

When choosing your lighting you must take into account not only the level and type of brightness, but also the heat that will be released.

Cornice lighting allows you to illuminate downward using light sources concealed behind a masonry cornice located at the point where the ceiling meets the wall.

It is natural light that is most appreciated by interior designers. The sources of natural light in houses should always be used to the maximum effect.

Skylights or fanlights are a traditional way to take advantage of the natural light that the roof of a house receives, which is usually wasted.

Almost the whole surface of the front wall of this house has been filled with large windows in order to make the most effective use of the natural light.

In this case, the windows occupying an entire wall do not just have a utilitarian function—to take advantage of the natural light—but also a decorative one, acting as a frame for the spectacular landscape.

Fixed windows cannot be opened to
ventilate the room, so their sole function is
to provide light to the interior of the home.

The windows of this house provide a sufficient level of general light and leave the direct and additional lighting to the built-in directional spotlights in the false ceiling.

Translucent curtains enable you to tone down the level of light entering through the windows, reducing or increasing its intensity depending on whether they are open or closed.

Color and light

7

8

9

10

1 Windows built high into the wall of the house are normally used as a source of extra lighting when it is considered that the level of light provided by conventional windows will not be sufficient.

2 You can make good use of the wall in the gable roof by creating a triangular window.

3 A curved window occupying an entire wall separates the living room from the terrace of this house with a gable roof. The grid of horizontal and vertical elements visually transforms it into a grid of light.

4 An indoor patio does not provide as much light as a window completely open to the outside, but it still should not be rejected out of hand. It will increase the sense of space and provide visual "air."

5 A roof of translucent panels provides brightness in the library of this home.

6 Two armchairs beside a small coffee table serve to create an inviting reading area bathed in natural light.

7 The upper half of the glass wall of this room has been frosted to tone down and reduce the quantity of natural light entering through it.

8 Dormer windows are vertical windows in the upright section built into a sloping roof.

9 The window above the kitchen sink allows those working there to see outside and also provides unbeatable clear light.

10 Windows like these enable you to take advantage of the height of the partitions to illuminate adjacent spaces. Their swivel-mounted frames also allow you to regulate the passage of air.

The small fixed circular window positioned above the main window of this living room provides extra brightness to the room and compensates for the visual heaviness of the brick wall.

The pavement lights in the floor of this platform (effectively a window cut out horizontally) also allow the light to reach the lower level.

Windows also have a decorative purpose. The skylights in this monumental space generate the effect of sunlight on the walls.

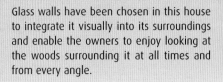

Glass walls have been chosen in this house to integrate it visually into its surroundings and enable the owners to enjoy looking at the woods surrounding it at all times and from every angle.

A window placed high up will enable the light to reach a greater distance than one at medium height, although it will leave the area below it in partial shadow.

The various forms of the windows and sources of artificial light in this space (rectangular, oblong, semicircular, square, and spherical) give it dynamism.

PHOTOGRAPHIC CREDITS[1]

A. Burckhardt, B. Santo pp. 226 (4), 352 (6)

Adam Butler pp. 14 (2), 127, 231, 301, 307 (7), 353 (10), 384, 403 (8), 435 (9), 468

Adrian Gregorutti pp. 46, 134, 190, 264 (1), 499

Ake E:son Liedman pp. 16, 137, 248, 263, 344, 383, 390, 398, 400

Alessandro Ciampi pp. 54, 109 (7), 434 (6), 478

Alberto Martínez pp. 15 (9), 64 (2), 71, 53 (10), 230, 365 (10)

Alberto Peris Caminero pp. 27, 36 (4), 50 (1), 80 (5), 358 (2),

Alberto Piovano pp. 37 (7), 264 (4), 314, 487 (8)

Alejandro Bahamón (architect) pp. 53, 65 (10), 227 (7), 277 (9), 279, 324, 388 (2), 486 (6)

Ah Bekman, Salib Kucuktuna (architect) pp. 37 (8), 216, 221, 347

Andrea Martiradonna pp. 42 (6), 43 (8, 10), 56 (6), 67, 69, 79, 145, 182, 189 (7), 194 (5), 206 (6), 245, 295, 309, 373, (9), 387, 477 (8, 10), 506–507

Andreas Greber Hasle-Ruegsau p. 318 (6)

Andrés Ortero pp. 343 (7), 422

Andrew Wood pp. 14 (3), 21 (8), 88, 114, 169 (10), 237, 320, 342 (2)

Angel Baltanás pp. 64 (5), 171, 175 (8), 372 (4)

Angelo Destefani pp. 29 (8), 226 (2), 272, 354, 366

Azcue pp. 414 (4)

Barclay & Crousse pp. 24 (2), 37 (10), 223

Benny Chan/Fotoworks pp. 50 (5), 156, 191, 397 (9), 403 (7), 414 (1)

Bill Timmerman pp. 15 (10), 148 (6), 200 (6), 222, 235, 501

Calor-color p. 482

Caramel Architekten pp. 206 (2), 504 (6)

Carlos Dominguez pp. 28 (6), 217, 257, 268, 308, 319 (9), 333, 353 (7), 364 (6), 372 (5), 405, 476 (3)

Carlos Emilio p. 149 (10)

Christian Richters pp. 56 (2), 64 (1), 94–95, 131 (8), 296 (4)

Christopher Wesnofske pp. 34, 51 (8), 296 (3)

Claudia Uribe pp. 130 (3), 179, 252 (3), 318 (3), 346

Cog Work Shop, Deborah Bird pp. 41, 66, 330 (1)

Dao Lou Zha p. 183

David Joseph pp. 19, 142, 494

Davide Virdis pp. 42 (3), 104–105, 338, 365 (8), 454

Dear p. 413

Deidi von Schaewen/Omnia pp. 219, 376 (1, 6), 377 (7, 8), 462, 464-465

Dominique Vorillon pp. 73, 242 (4), 255, 260, 278, 280, 359 (8), 371

Duravit pp. 194 (1, 3, 4), 195 (9), 215, 388 (6)

Edua Wilde pp. 74 (3), 296 (1), 328

Eduard Hueber/Archpboto pp. 97, 108 (1,5), 130 (4), 135, 205, 242 (5), 276 (3), 317, 402 (3), 489

Eduardo Consuegra pp. 372 (3)

Eugeni Pons pp. 14 (4), 23, 26, 57 (10), 70, 74 (6), 75 (8), 107, 352 (1), 365 (9), 457 (8, 9), 477 (7), 491, 504 (1, 4)

Flaminia pp. 192, 194 (2), 201 (9), 212–213

Foscarini p. 483

Francesca Giovanelli pp. 163 (8), 299, 312, 510

Future-Scape Architects, Daigo Ishi pp. 334, 341, 343 (10),

Gary Chang, Janet Choy pp. 56 (4), 152, 184 (4), 188 (2), 415 (10)

Gianni Basso/Vega MG p. 140

Giorgio Baroni pp. 141, 186, 238, 274-275, 319 (10), 321, 322, 342 (3), 348, 367, 375, 376 (5), 392, 492 (6)

Graft pp. 130 (1)

Groep Delta Architectuur pp. 225, 227 (10), 250, 495

Gus Wüstemann p. 486 (3)

Guy Objin pp. 224, 226 (3), 388 (5), 389 (9), 396 (4), 434 (3)

Hans Peter Wörndl pp. 331 (8), 376 (3), 389 (8)

Hanspeter Schiess p. 100

Hervé Abbadie pp. 74 (2), 75 (10), 81 (10), 109 (8), 121, 241, 253 (8), 276 (5), 294, 335, 352 (5), 426, 484

Hiroyuki Hirai pp. 36 (2), 148 (1), 342 (1)

Ignacio Martínez pp. 20 (4), 86, 124, 139, 174 (6), 185 (9), 276 (2), 313, 401, 496

J. Latova pp. 188 (1), 226 (1), 252 (1), 318 (2), 503, 504 (5)

Jacques Dirand p. 162 (4)

James Silverman pp. 25 (10), 130 (5), 148 (2), 242 (1), 252 (4), 345, 403 (9)

James Wilkins p. 206 (5)

Jeroen Dellensen pp. 132,184 (5), 325, 342 (5)

Joan Mundó pp. 28 (1), 246, 357, 437

João Ribeiro pp. 52, 72, 161, 266, 327, 362

John Ellis pp. 31, 352 (2, 3), 148 (5), 185 (7), 226 (6), 353 (9)

Jordi Miralles pp. 2, 14 (1), 20 (3), 28 (3), 29 (9), 43 (7), 47, 56 (5), 57 (7), 58–59, 74 (4, 5), 80 (3), 92 (2, 3, 5), 108 (3), 125, 130 (2, 6), 133, 154, 158, 168 (3), 178, 200 (2), 207 (8), 208–209, 228–229, 253 (7, 9, 10), 264 (5, 6), 267, 271, 276 (6), 285, 290–292, 296 (2, 5), 306 (1), 307 (8), 316, 330 (3, 5), 331 (9, 10), 343 (8), 360, 364 (1, 3), 372 (2,4), 391, 402 (6), 434 (2, 4), 435 (8, 10), 436, 438–439, 445, 455, 456 (2, 4), 457 (10), 458–459, 471, 485, 487 (7), 488, 490, 492 (5), 493 (9), 502

Jordi Sarrá pp. 20 (1, 6), 24 (3, 5, 6), 25 (7), 29 (7), 42 (2, 4), 60, 80 (6), 83, 91, 98–99, 103, 106, 108 (6), 111–113, 115–119, 123, 129, 146, 168 (2, 5), 169 (7, 9), 174 (2), 175 (7, 8), 181, 188 (4), 193, 196, 199, 200 (3, 5), 201 (10), 202, 204, 214, 273, 286, 306 (6), 307 (9, 10), 358 (3, 6), 370, 372 (6), 373 (7), 376 (4), 377 (10), 381–382, 388 (4), 389 (7, 10), 393–395, 396 (2, 5), 397 (8), 410–411, 414 (3, 6), 417–421, 423–425, 427–432, 440, 442–443, 448–453, 456 (3), 463, 466–467, 475, 481

José Luis Hausmann pp. 120, 144, 148 (4), 160, 206 (1), 252 (5), 358 (5s), 397 (7), 433, 479

Jovan Horvát pp. 340, 396 (3), 415 (9)

Joy von Tiedemann pp. 96, 110, 184 (1), 304, 330 (4), 476 (5)

Juan Rodríguez pp. 50 (2), 57 (8), 128, 207 (10)

Karin Hessmann/Artur p. 81 (9)

Kinder Räume p. 330 (6)

Knott Architects pp. 84, 131 (10), 184 (2), 486 (5)

Kouji Okamoto pp. 18, 40

L. Agnoletto, M. Rusconi p. 339

Laurent Brandajs pp. 14 (6), 15 (7), 50 (3), 51 (9), 80 (1, 4), 93 (9), 108 (4), 138, 149 (9), 151, 194 (6), 195 (7), 206 (4), 242 (2, 3, 6), 243 (8), 251, 259, 265 (7), 277 (8), 302, 306 (4), 319 (7), 330 (2), 386, 399, 476 (4), 477 (9), 486 (2), 487 (9), 492 (1)

Linda Vismara/Vega MG p. 388 (3)

Luigi Filetici pp. 155, 168 (6)

Luis Asin pp. 28 (5), 50 (4), 56 (3), 166, 297 (7)

Luis Hevia pp. 16, 21 (10), 51 (10), 68, 169 (8), 414 (6), 434 (5)

Luis Ros pp. 470, 472

Lyndon Douglas pp. 187, 493 (7)

Matteo Piazza pp. 28 (2), 29 (10), 35, 43 (9), 44, 57 (9), 74 (1), 82, 220, 240, 270, 276 (4), 277 (10), 288, 297 (8, 9, 10) 353 (8), 376 (2), 447, 456 (1,6), 476 (1), 480, 487 (10), 492 (4), 511

Michael Freisager Fotografie pp. 21 (7), 37 (9), 188 (5)

Michael Moran pp. 20 (2), 36 (5), 64 (3), 65 (8), 78, 108 (2), 247

Michel De Vita pp. 81 (8), 174 (1), 189 (10), 298

Miquel Tres pp. 203, 249, 283, 358 (1), 359 (10), 414 (5), 434 (1)

Miri Davidovitch pp. 15 (8), 32, 77, 252 (6), 264 (2)

Montse Garriga pp. 50 (6), 365 (7)

Nacasa & Partners Inc. p. 385

Nelson Kon pp. 48, 64 (4)

Nick Philbedge pp. 55, 157, 504 (3)

Nuria Fuentes pp. 102, 207 (9), 351, 474, 476 (6)

Pablo Rojas, Alvaro Gutiérrez pp. 162 (6), 168 (1), 170, 200 (1)

Page Goolrick pp. 80 (2), 162 (1)

Paul Ott pp. 22, 90, 189 (9), 210–211, 261, 281, 306 (5), 364 (5), 368

Paul Rivera/Archphoto pp. 76, 147,164, 188 (3), 207 (7), 236, 256, 388 (1)

Pedro D'Orey pp. 45, 300, 355, 358 (4), 380, 509

Pekka Littow pp. 21 (9), 65 (7), 318 (1), 402 (1), 505 (8)

Pep Escoda pp. 13, 64 (6), 81 (7), 85, 258, 264 (3), 277 (7), 310, 361, 396 (1), 412, 444, 469, 476 (2)

Peter Wenger pp. 51 (7), 92 (1), 143, 276 (1), 504 (2)

Pizzi and Thompson pp. 25 (9), 42 (5), 226 (5), 227 (9)

René Pedersen p. 185 (10)

Richard Dean p. 162 (5)

Richard Glover p. 435 (7)

Rika Oishi p. 149 (8)

Robert Shimer Hedrig Blessing pp. 284, 315, 500

Rupert Steiner pp. 42 (1), 75 (9), 92 (4), 93 (8), 122, 185 (8), 188 (6), 201 (8), 244, 323, 493 (8)

Ryota Atarashi pp. 101, 311, 486 (1)

Santiago Barrio pp. 65 (9), 234, 252 (2), 296 (6), 364 (4), 374, 505 (7)

Satoshi Asakawa pp. 20 (5), 36 (1, 6)

Satoshi Okada Architects pp. 262, 508

Scott Frances pp. 49, 62–63, 175 (9), 184 (6), 200 (4), 350, 352 (4), 377 (9), 404, 473

Seong Kwon pp. 136, 201 (7), 243 (9), 359 (7, 9), 397 (10), 505 (10)

Shania Shegedyn pp. 28 (4), 30, 126, 165, 227 (8), 254

Shannon McGrath p. 372 (1)

Sharrin Rees pp. 93 (7), 131 (9), 150, 162 (3), 163 (10), 167, 174 (4), 175 (10), 195 (8), 306 (3), 318 (4), 343 (9), 373(8), 446, 486 (4), 492 (2), 493 (10)

Solvi dos Santos/Omnia pp. 168 (4), 457 (7)

Steffen Jänicke, Jens Vogt pp. 36 (3), 176–177, 184 (3)

Stephan Zähring p. 174 (3)

Steve Williams pp. 87, 265 (10), 329

Tim Griffith pp. 56 (1), 342 (6), 415 (8)

Tisettanta p. 441

Toni Leichner pp. 131 (7), 148 (3), 206 (3)

Tuca Reinés pp. 75 (7), 189 (8), 305, 319 (8), 492 (3)

Undine Pröhl pp. 109 (9), 153, 163 (7), 172–173, 174 (5), 243 (7), 265 (8), 282, 336, 402 (2, 4), 403 (10)

Verycruisse Dujardin p. 149 (7)

Vincent Knapp p. 195 (10)

Virginia del Giudice p. 373 (10)

Weberhaus p. 318 (6)

Weldon Brewster pp. 17, 61, 406–407, 498

Yael Pincus pp. 12, 14 (5), 24 (1, 5), 25 (8), 33, 38–39, 92 (6), 109 (10), 159, 162 (2), 163 (9), 180, 197, 198, 218, 239, 243 (10), 265 (9), 269, 287, 293, 303, 306 (2), 318 (5), 331 (7), 332, 342 (4), 349, 356, 363, 364 (2), 369, 378–379, 396 (6), 402 (5), 414 (2), 415 (7), 416, 456 (5), 460–461, 497, 505 (9)

Yong Kwan Kim pp. 89, 289, 326, 337

[1]The numbers in brackets indicate the photograph.